Austrian Economic Perspectives on Individualism and Society

Austrian Economic Perspectives on Individualism and Society

Moving Beyond Methodological Individualism

Edited by

Guinevere Liberty Nell

palgrave
macmillan

AUSTRIAN ECONOMIC PERSPECTIVES ON INDIVIDUALISM AND SOCIETY

First published in 2014 by PALGRAVE MACMILLAN® in the United States—a division of St. Martin's Press LLC, 175 Fifth Avenue, New York, NY 10010.

Where this book is distributed in the UK, Europe and the rest of the world, this is by Palgrave Macmillan, a division of Macmillan Publishers Limited, registered in England, company number 785998, of Houndmills, Basingstoke, Hampshire RG21 6XS.

Palgrave Macmillan is the global academic imprint of the above companies and has companies and representatives throughout the world.

ISBN: 978-1-137-37140-9

Library of Congress Cataloging-in-Publication Data

Austrian economic perspectives on individualism and society : moving beyond methodological individualism / edited by Guinevere Liberty Nell.
pages cm
Includes bibliographical references and index.
ISBN 978-1-137-37140-9 (hardcover : alk. paper)
1. Austrian school of economics. 2. Individualism. I. Nell, Guinevere Liberty, 1976-
HB98.A955 2014
330.15'7—dc23

2014021994

A catalogue record of the book is available from the British Library.

Design by Amnet.

First edition: November 2014

10 9 8 7 6 5 4 3 2 1

Contents

List of Figures and Tables

INTRODUCTION

Economists are frequently criticized for seeing the world through the narrow lens of the economic, seeing individuals as purely self-interested and profit seeking, and failing to see the importance of community. Even economists recognize these failings, and new branches of economics like behaviorism have been introduced in part to address them. However, neoclassical economics, including Austrian economics, still relies upon incentives based in self-interest, and the rooting of all behavior in *individual* action and preferences, in order to model and predict outcomes.

Is this defensible, necessary, and right? Are there any alternative ways to model behavior that are consistent with Austrian theory? What are the pitfalls of relying upon methodological individualism and self-interest, and of neglecting community or underestimating the importance of society and culture?

In putting together this volume, which is a kind of follow-up to the collection I put together on *Austrian Theory and Economic Organization* published in August 2014, I expected to be flooded with potential contributors, since the subject is so important and so interesting. To my surprise, there was significantly less interest in this book than in the other. Why should this be? The reasons given ranged from "everything on that subject has already been said" to what seemed like concerns that saying anything new on the subject might take the theorist outside the framework of Austrian theory and methodology, which is grounded in *individual* action. Hence, this collection presents the thoughts of just six Austrian-inspired economists willing to burst out from those boundaries and seek answers only visible when Austrian theory is open to the insights of other (generally heterodox) schools, or when critically analyzing the foundations of Austrian theory.

This volume brings together a wide spectrum of theoretical angles, all inspired by or in conversation with Austrian economics, to explore these questions and consider possible routes to a more well-developed view of humanity and society, which might in turn help to build foundations for further explorations of the organizational topics raised in the first volume. The first section tackles methodological individualism head-on, exploring Friedrich Hayek's view and the shift in the school from the views of early Austrian Ludwig von Mises to that of Hayek. Did Mises ground the school too much in the individual, more so than the founder of the Austrian school, Carl Menger, would have wanted? This is impossible to know, but many Austrians today believe that Hayek, with his spontaneous order framework and his work on cognition, has given Austrian models a more dynamic and modern approach, which can be joined with Complex Adaptive Systems (CAS) theory. This is often the aspect of Austrian economics that other schools of economics see as promising.

If Austrian economics can shake its image as ideologically fixated upon laissez-faire, this dynamic and literary (nonmathematical) complexity may influence other schools and help lead them away from their simplistic assumptions about rational self-interest. Austrians who want other schools to see the benefit and potential of Austrian ways of thinking should explore the divergence between the Misesian framework rooted in *individual* "human action" and the more flexible "spontaneous order" framework that Hayek introduced, which need not be rooted solely in the individual.

In the first chapter, Andy Denis explores Hayek's views. He argues that Hayek is inconsistent. His earlier writings that introduce "the intentional stance," Denis argues, have much of interest, but his assertions of the individualist nature of his methodology depend on an erroneous division between nature and society. Later writings, in which the "intentional stance" is extended to the macro-economic level, avoid these errors, making his overall vision more consistent.

Gus diZerega (chapter 2) explores the shift among Austrian economists from the Misesian insistence upon a strict methodological individualism rooted in individual action to a dynamic macroeconomic spontaneous order-based framework. He argues that Hayek described the market as a complex adaptive system shaping "distributed knowledge" (knowledge known to no one in its entirety) through a process of discovery, and that such an order cannot be understood through the *a priori* logic of human action. Humans are social beings, and hence even freedom is a social concept. Social interactions must be available: being "free" on a desert island is not a realm of human freedom because human beings are "irreducibly social." Hence, diZerega argues that it is time to demote methodological individualism from its primary role in much of social science to just one (important) "moment" among three that shape society.

The second section explores spontaneous order and society. Nell (chapter 3) considers how recognition of the "social individual," that is, one who is shaped by society, changes the predicted outcomes within the spontaneous orders of society, including markets, culture, and democracy. If rational self-interest of individuals is not taken as the root of all action, can the assumptions and conclusions of the "public choice" school be defended? How does this change the direction that Austrian models should take? Expectations, habits, and culture are endogenous to the system: they emerge from the system itself. Culture affects an individual's "nature," including her habits, preferences, and the way she responds to the incentives of the system. Culture and custom may be more important than even the legal institutions, so a decentralized, evolving democratic system, with transparency and public conversation integrated and internal to the system and its coevolving culture, may produce far more efficient public programs, and the economy may not need to be laissez-faire to be growth promoting and poverty reducing, even according to Austrian models. The inclusion of a democratic process theory in addition to market process theory may allow Austrians to study this branch of inquiry.

Troy Camplin (chapter 4) fills out this section with a study of the various types of spontaneous orders in any given society, looking at cultures, civil society, and the orders "in-between." He argues that even those most dedicated to an individualistic worldview recognize that humans are social, but that this is not in conflict with human individuality. Instead, our sociality drives our individualism, and our individualism keeps societies dynamic. He argues that it is vital that we work to create the conditions for the emergence of healthy institutions (which are also kinds of self-organizing processes), which will support the emergence of healthy spontaneous orders, healthy cultures, and healthy civil societies, which requires existence of rule of law, flexible law over rigid legislation, freedom of entry and exit, and freedom of communication. Furthermore, he argues, culture can have a very strong impact on the nature of the institutions and spontaneous orders because culture can create "perverse orders."

The third and final section considers further implications for "mind and society." How does an approach recognizing that we are all interconnected and not merely rational self-interested individuals affect our views not only on culture and the economy but also on our understanding of ourselves? What does Hayek's work on cognition offer to our understanding of society? Corey Abel and Leslie Marsh (chapter 5) start off this section with a discussion of the theories of Hayek and Michael Oakeshott, and their understanding of liberty, mind, and society. This deep exploration offers a foundation for a more balanced and reasonable debate over the extent of liberty possible in a good society, as well as a more complex understanding of the individual actor within the society.

Finally, this section concludes with an exploration of Hayek's view on cognition (the "internal") and his views on society (the "external"), both viewed and framed as spontaneous orders, and the implications of this framing for analysis of the individual within society. Nell (chapter 6) discusses Hayek's "connectionist" philosophy of the emergence of the mind, and the relationship between the spontaneous order of the mind and the spontaneous orders of society. Psychological development of the mind is affected by society, and an individual's preferences and beliefs will be developed as a reflection of the society in which that mind resides.

The individualism of a market economy may be damaging in a different way than the more united but also more hierarchical planned economy. The complex system of the mind, like the complex system of the market, requires a free area in order to develop and evolve toward a well-functioning system. This cannot occur in a planned economy nor in a highly traditional system, for example, a strictly religious society, but how well can it occur in a free market economy? What affect might "consumerism" and other consequences of free markets have on the free development of the individual, freedom of thought and action, and on social relationships and community? What if human nature could change, not because institutions are changed by force, but because the evolution of both society and the individual occurred in a process of transformation of two interdependent complex adaptive systems? Nell explores these and related questions in the final chapter by connecting Hayek's spontaneous order theory and cognitive analysis to connectionist neural theory and developmental psychology.

Together, I hope that these essays open discussion among Austrians on the fundamental issue of whether the individual can really be treated in isolation, as the foundation of Austrian methodology and theory. Should the individual be seen as the originator of his or her preferences, or should individuals be seen as created by society as much as society is created by individuals? If the latter is the case, Austrians should consider whether and how this must change Austrian models. Finally, I hope that other heterodox economists and social scientists consider the Austrian approach, once this modification has been made.

PART 1

Surpassing Methodological Individualism

CHAPTER 1

METHODOLOGICAL INDIVIDUALISM AND SOCIETY: HAYEK'S EVOLVING VIEW

ANDY DENIS, CITY UNIVERSITY LONDON

INTRODUCTION

A core topic of the present volume is the methodologically individualist approach of the Austrian School. In particular, we are concerned to understand how—and whether—this individualistic methodology can help us to understand the workings of society. To address this we turn in this chapter to Friedrich Hayek's lucid discussion of the matter in the *Economica* articles published during the Second World War (Hayek 1942, 1943, 1944) and subsequently collected in the *Counter-Revolution of Science* (1979), first published in 1952. We are particularly concerned with chapters 3 and 4, "The Subjective Character of the Social Sciences" and "The Individualist and 'Compositive' Method of the Social Sciences" (1979: 41–60 and 61–76). The conclusion drawn is that there is much to commend Hayek's vision of the operation of social science—indeed this is a sophisticated and illuminating discussion. Nevertheless, it is marred by his methodological individualism—the idea that social science must start with parts and reconstitute the whole, while natural science starts with wholes and by analysis attempts to retrieve the parts. A particular feature of Hayek's discussion is his deployment of what Daniel Dennett has come to call the "intentional stance." A discussion of Hayek's application of this approach to social evolution in his later works shows how he himself breaks with the mistaken precepts of his individualist methodology. Other chapters in this volume, particularly those by diZerega and Nell, also take up aspects of Hayek's intellectual journey, which led him to question or abandon elements of traditional Austrian methodology.

Subjectivity and the Individual—Hayek's Early Methodological Stance

Hayek begins his account by setting out the view that the goal of social science is to explain the unintended consequences of human action, which itself has to be understood as taking place within a network of social relations: "social studies . . . deal . . . with the relations between men and things or the relations between man and man. They are concerned with man's actions, and the aim is to explain the unintended or undesigned results of the actions of many men" (41). The aspect of human action with which we are concerned is choice: "The social sciences . . . are concerned with man's conscious or reflected action, actions where a person can be said to choose between various courses open to him" (42–43). This aspect of the study of society—which for Hayek is foundational—is accessible to us because we can resort to *Verstehen*: "We know . . . that in his conscious decisions man classifies external stimuli in a way which we know solely from our own subjective experience" (43). So when we study the unintended consequences of human action, we can understand the behavior of the mass, of "many men," because when they make their choices they base them on a classification of stimuli—an understanding of their interaction with their environment—which we can understand by virtue of our own subjective experience.

In adopting this stance—one that I wholeheartedly endorse—Hayek places the application of what Dennett refers to as the "intentional stance" at the core of the investigation of society. To do otherwise, Hayek says, would be "impossible" (44). Dennett explains the intentional stance as follows:

> first you decide to treat the object whose behavior is to be predicted as a rational agent; then you figure out what beliefs that agent ought to have, given its place in the world and its purpose. Then you figure out what desires it ought to have, on the same considerations, and finally you predict that this rational agent will act to further its goals in the light of its beliefs. A little practical reasoning from the chosen set of beliefs and desires will in most instances yield a decision about what the agent ought to do; that is what you predict the agent will do. (1996: 17)

This is Hayek's procedure. He focuses on the individual economic agent, considering both his goals and his beliefs about the likely consequences of his actions, given his place in the world, that is, his location within a network of relationships.

Hayek underlines that the social entities that we study and are to explain are socially valid abstractions. Such entities are "abstractions from all the physical attributes of the things in question . . . their definition must run entirely in terms of mental attitudes of men." They exist—that is, they have social validity—because people believe that they exist: "most of the objects of social or human action are not 'objective facts' . . . and they cannot at all be defined in physical terms. So far as human actions are concerned the things *are* what the acting people think they are" (44).

Up to this point, Hayek has quickly sketched a profoundly sophisticated vision in which the objects of social science are socially valid entities, determined by mental attitudes of economic agents, but arising behind their backs as unintended consequences of their choices. But this immediately raises an interesting issue: "The objects or the 'facts' of the social sciences are also opinions . . . opinions of those whose actions produce the objects of the social scientist" (47). So agents have opinions, and these opinions both *are* the facts of social science and *produce* the facts of social science. The facts of social science are both cause and effect—the beliefs that lead to action, and the actions that then lead to beliefs. So should we regard social facts as objective or subjective? These social facts "are thus as little 'subjective' as those of the natural sciences, because they are independent of the particular observer" (47). "But in another sense . . . the facts of the social sciences are merely opinions, views held by the people whose actions we study" (47). They are both subjective and objective, views held by people en masse, but independent of the will of individuals—that is, they are socially valid abstractions.

Thus, according to Hayek, beliefs "as such are our data, irrespective of whether they are true or false . . . moreover, we cannot directly observe [them] in the minds of the people but . . . we can recognize [them] from what they do and say merely because we have ourselves a mind similar to theirs" (47). To underline this point, Hayek adds that even when we bring physical reality into play, it can only exert an influence via its effect on consciousness: "all the 'physical laws of production' which we meet, for example, in economics, are not physical laws in the sense of the physical sciences, but people's beliefs about what they can do" (52). Hence "the relations between men . . . for the purposes of social study cannot be defined in the objective terms of the social sciences but only in terms of human beliefs" (52). The content of social science is simply and purely belief: "Not only man's action toward external objects but also all the relations between men and all the social institutions can be understood only by what men think about them" (57).

Hayek describes this as "the subjectivist approach of the social sciences," and in his view "every important advance in economic theory during the last hundred years was a further step in the consistent application of subjectivism" in this sense: "Society as we know it is, as it were, built up from the concepts and ideas held by the people; and social phenomena can be recognized by us and have meaning to us only as they are reflected in the minds of men" (58). Society is "built up" of socially valid ideas, ideas, and beliefs that have validity, that is, social efficacy, regardless of their objective truth, and it is the job of the social scientist to retrace that building up by connecting these ideas to reconstitute the social structure, the unintended consequence of human decisions. But "it is . . . the individual concepts, the views people have formed of each other and of the things, which form the true elements of the social structure" (58).

These mutual beliefs constitute relationships between people, and it is the network of these relationships in which the individual is embedded and within which he makes his decisions: "If the social structure can remain the same although different individuals succeed each other at particular points, this is not because the individuals which succeed each other are completely identical, but because they succeed each other in particular relations. . . . The individuals are merely the *foci* in the network of relationships" (59). The nodes or focuses of the networks of relations are social roles, occupied by individuals.

The social structure is thus a set of social relations, a "network of relationships" within which individuals are embedded, and which leads to similarity, or at least congruence, of individual behavior, such that the social structure "remains the same," despite changes of personnel. Individuals succeed each other within that set of relations, that is, they inherit roles.

The relationships between people are constituted by the "attitudes they take toward other people" and the "particular views held by other people about them"—"it is the various attitudes of the individuals toward each other . . . which form the recurrent, recognizable and familiar elements of the structure." So the social relationships are the mutual expectations that agents have of each other—expectations that themselves depend upon the roles that individuals play. Hayek gives the example of a policeman. The expectations he has of others, and the expectations that they have of him—*in his role as a policeman*, those "which are relevant to his function as policeman . . . preserve a constant structural element which can be separated and studied in isolation" (59).

This is a profound and sophisticated account. But recall that the goal is to explain the unintended macro-level consequences of individual action.

Hayek at this point, toward the end of chapter 3, now introduces a very important and subtle consequence of what he has said so far:

> While we can recognize these elements of human relationships only because they are known to us from the working of our own minds, this does not mean that the *significance* of their combination in a particular pattern relating different individuals must be immediately obvious to us. It is only by the systematic and patient following up of the *implications* of many people holding certain views that we can understand . . . the unintended and often uncomprehended *results* of the separate yet interrelated actions of men in society." (59, my emphasis)

So we can use *Verstehen* to understand why people do what they do—the choices they make and so forth, but the wider social significance of those actions in the form of a pattern of relationships relating the individuals in society, that is, the unintended consequences of those choices, cannot be understood in the same way. They are unintended, so our empathy with others' goals and intentions is of no assistance. So how are we to understand them? The answer is, by the exercise of the synthetic power of the mind. At this point this is stated in general terms, indicating merely the "systematic and patient following up" of the implications of belief, and the "effort to reconstruct these different patterns of social relations." The question is addressed more fully in the next chapter, on "The Individualist and 'Compositive' method of the Social Sciences" (Hayek, 1979: 61–76).

Hayek starts his discussion of methodological individualism per se, or the individualist method, with the idea that the entities that social scientists study, socially valid ideas, appear twice: "The special difficulties of the social sciences, and much confusion about their character, derive precisely from the fact that in them ideas appear in two capacities, as it were, as part of their object, and as ideas about that object" (61). In social sciences, he says, "it is necessary to draw a distinction between those ideas which are *constitutive* of the phenomena we want to explain and the ideas which either we ourselves or the very people whose actions we have to explain may have formed *about* these phenomena and which are not the cause of, but theories about the social structures" (62).

This is particularly important because the people whose behavior we are studying "form ideas about the undesigned results of their actions—popular theories about the various social structures or formations" (62). "The real contrast is between ideas which by being held by the people become the cause of a social phenomenon and the ideas which people form about that phenomenon" (62–63). It is important to distinguish between "the motivating or constitutive opinions on the one hand and speculative or explanatory views which people have formed" (64) on the other. So not only are individual agents driven by mutual expectations in making the choices they make, but they also form ideological views about the unintended consequences of those choices—a folk political economy, as it were. And those views will also influence the choices that people make. It is the task of the social scientist to expose what is true and what is false in these folk conceptions: "our study has to revise and improve" them.

For Hayek, there is a further dimension, and that dimension is critically important for our investigation. He identifies constitutive ideas as ideas that constitute the behavior of the individual person, the choices that he makes. We have already seen this in the discussion up to this point. The ideas that the policeman, and those with whom he comes into contact, hold about his behavior and the way others will respond to his actions, are constitutive of his choices. They are the constant structural component that is the object of social science. But the notions of folk political economy concern social "wholes." This is because they are folk explanations of the unintended consequences of individual action for the society—they are about the social structure or social formation that emerges undesignedly from individual choice. They are about "the causes of [a] change in price or about the 'nature of value' in general . . . ideas they may have formed about the whole of 'society,' or the 'economic system,' to which they belong" (63).

So the "popular mind" may form ideas about "such collectives as society or the economic system," but the social scientist must "refrain from treating these pseudo-entities as facts," and "systematically start from the concepts which guide individuals in their actions" (64). Starting instead from the proposed higher-level entities treats "as facts those collectives which are no more than popular generalizations" (65). This, according to Hayek, betrays a "collectivist prejudice" (65).

There is a jump here, a hiatus in the logical train of thought. It may be true that a scientific explanation of some phenomenon unintended by the human agents whose action underpins it is incomplete until it has been shown to be consistent with some set of choices and hence with a set of constitutive ideas. But that certainly does not mean that an analysis of such a set of phenomena is necessarily either false or useless until it has that quality of completeness. Moreover, it may not be possible to get to the explanation of the unintended consequence starting with the behavior of individuals. Two discussions that Hayek engages in elsewhere are relevant here.

At the end of *The Sensory Order*, in the chapter on "Philosophical Consequences," in the section on "Dualism and Materialism," Hayek says the following about the relationship between our studies of the "microcosm," or the physical world, and the corresponding "macrocosm," or mental world:

> While our theory leads us to deny any ultimate dualism of the forces governing the realms of mind and that of the physical world respectively, it forces us at the same time to recognize that for practical purposes we shall always have to adopt a dualistic view. . . . [A]ny explanation of mental phenomena which we can hope ever to attain cannot be sufficient to "unify" all our knowledge, in the sense that we should become able to substitute statements about particular physical events (or classes of physical events) for statements about mental event. . . . [W]e shall never be able to bridge the gap between physical and mental phenomena; and for practical purposes . . . we shall permanently have to be content with a dualistic view of the world. (1952: 179)

Again, earlier in *The Counter-Revolution of Science*, Hayek makes the same point. Discussing the study of individual choice and its social consequences, he says that "The external stimulus which may be said to cause or occasion such actions can of course also be defined in purely physical terms. But if we tried to do so for the purposes of explaining human action, we would confine ourselves to less than we know about the situation" (1979: 43).

Let us try to apply the same mode of thought to the relationship between the social microcosm—the individual making choices embedded within a network of social relationships, and the corresponding macrocosm—the unintended social outcomes of such decision-making, including the network of social relationships itself. Then we might say that although there is no ultimate dualism between micro and macro, it may be that—perhaps for the foreseeable future—we have to adopt a dualistic view. An explanation of social phenomena that we can hope currently to attain cannot be sufficient to "unify" all our knowledge, in the sense that we should become able to substitute statements about particular individual choice events (or classes of such events) for statements about social events. In our discussion of social events, to attempt to confine ourselves to individual events is to confine ourselves to less than we know. At the very least, if this strategy is not open to us, it is up to Hayek to explain why that is so. We will have more to say on this in the sequel.

For Hayek, therefore, we must start with the micro, the socially embedded individual, and build up the macro therefrom. Hayek thus implicitly endorses a version of the microfoundations project. In the social sciences

> it is the concepts and views held by individuals which are directly known to us and which form the elements from which we must build up, as it

> were, the more complex phenomena . . . it is the attitudes of individuals which are the familiar elements and by the combination of which we try to reproduce the complex phenomena, the results of individual actions, which are much less known—a procedure which often leads to the discovery of principles of structural coherence of the complex phenomena which had not been (and perhaps could not be) established by direct observation. (65)

The natural sciences, in contrast, "necessarily begin with the complex phenomena of nature and work backward to infer the elements from which they are composed" (65–66). Hayek thus regards the difference between the social and natural sciences as expressing a part-whole relation:

> The place where the human individual stands in the order of things brings it about that in one direction what he perceives are the comparatively complex phenomena which he analyzes, while in the other direction what are given to him are elements from which those more complex phenomena are composed that he cannot observe as wholes. While the method of the natural sciences is in this sense, analytic, the method of the social sciences is better described as compositive or synthetic. (66–67)

In the social sciences, in Hayek's view, we only learn about totalities by means of synthesis, the "compositive" method, by systematically "fitting together" the elements, which are the mutual expectations of agents, to construct the entity in the mind: "It is the so-called wholes, the groups of elements which are structurally connected, which we learn to single out from the totality of observed phenomena only as a result to our systematic fitting together of the elements with familiar properties, and which we build up or reconstruct from the known properties of the elements" (67).

So for the social sciences, we follow methodological individualism—we start with the known intended actions in the context of the set or relationships determining mutual expectations of the economic agents and build up from there to reconstruct the resultant unknown and unintended social totalities. We derive "laws of the macrocosm" from our "knowledge of the microcosm" and these laws "always remain 'deductive'" because of "limited knowledge of the data of the complex situation" (72–73). For the natural sciences, we adopt the opposite path of methodological holism and start with the known wholes, proceeding by analysis to retrieve the unknown parts.

In my view we cannot accept Hayek's proposal to partition the world into a nonsocial field, in which we proceed by analysis, and a social one, in which we proceed by synthesis. Karl Marx, too, seems to privilege synthesis, although for different reasons: synthesis, he says, "is obviously the scientifically correct method" (1973: 101). In reality, science in both fields consists of a continual alternation between analysis and synthesis. Reality as it presents itself to us is always a complex unity of many determinations. We progress by analyzing what we see into simpler categories, which we then mentally recombine to reproduce the concrete as mentally concrete (1973: 101). The botanist sees the individual plants, or perhaps, from a distance, the woodland, fields, and so on, without discerning the individual organisms. He does not see species or phyla, or photosynthesis or respiration. These totalities have to be continually reconstructed in thought via analysis and synthesis. Hayek's view, taken literally, would imply that the social scientist can never see the wood for the trees, and the natural scientist the trees for the wood.

To take the behavior of the economic agent: He may make marginal choices to work, or to borrow, but these choices depend on the presence of opportunities to work and to borrow, and those opportunities—the structure of the incentives facing him—depend upon the operation of the labor and credit markets. The behavior of the agent cannot be understood except in the context of the dense network of social relations within which he is embedded. Hayek knows that the network of relationships cannot be reduced to a logically prior asocial individual. But equally it cannot be reduced to the individual choice—choice in his vision is social choice and depends upon social context. He says explicitly that it is the social context, the network of relations that can be separated and studied "in isolation." But then he falls back on the notion of "starting" from the individual—because the individual is said to be what we already know, because we have a mind like his. But the context, the network of relationships is not something we know initially—it has to be deduced from what people do and reconstructed in our thought. Hayek here is inconsistent.

The Theory of the Evolution of Society: Hayek's Later Shift Away from Methodological Individualism

Nor can we accept Hayek's proposal, implicit in these passages, to apply the intentional stance only to individual humans. Indeed, in his writing on the evolution of social institutions he goes further. In Hayek's theory of social evolution, the social context within which the socially embedded individual acts is codified as a "system of rules of individual conduct," and the unintended social consequence of his decisions according to that system of rules of individual conduct is the "overall order of the actions of a group of individuals" (Hayek, 1967: 67–68):

> *transmission* of rules of conduct takes place *from individual to individual*, while what may be called the natural *selection* of rules will operate on the basis of the greater or lesser efficiency of the resulting *order of the group*. . . . The evolutionary selection of different rules of individual conduct operates through the viability of the order it will produce." (1967: 68, emphasis in original)

Because this "overall order" is unintended, it is also often uncomprehended. It is what the members of the social group depend upon for their livelihoods, and in order to survive they must sustain it. But they do not know that. The rules of conduct that guide a society are functional, according to Hayek. Individuals must behave so as to preserve those functions, but they will not necessarily be able to understand them:

> the "functions" which these rules serve we shall be able to discover only after we have reconstructed the overall order which is produced by actions in accordance with them . . . all the individuals of the species which exist will behave in that manner because groups of individuals which have thus behaved have displaced those which did not do so. (Hayek, 1967: 70)

So we have a situation quite different from what we started with, in the *Counter-Revolution of Science*. There, the individual did what he did, motivated by his own interests, and according to what he thought the consequences would be for those interests from acting in particular ways. These actions had unintended social consequences, but no attention was given to the consequences to all the individuals from these social outcomes. Now, in *Philosophy, Politics and Economics*, we have a second rationality running alongside that of the individual agents. The "overall order of actions of the group" determines the fate of the individuals. Hayek expresses this second rationality as

> a sort of inversion of the relation between cause and effect in the sense that the structures possessing a kind of order will exist because the elements do what is necessary to secure the persistence of that order. The "final cause" or "purpose," i.e., the adaptation of the parts to the requirements of the whole, becomes a necessary part of the explanation of why structures of the kind exist: we are bound to explain the fact that the elements behave in a certain way by the circumstance than this sort of conduct is more likely to preserve the whole—on the preservation of which depends the preservation of the individuals, which would therefore not exist if they did not behave in this manner. A "teleological" explanation is thus entirely in order so long as it does not imply design by a maker but merely the recognition that the kind of structure would not have perpetuated itself if it did not

> act in a manner likely to produce certain effects, and that it has evolved through those prevailing at each stage who did. (77)

The social structure persists because the human elements of that structure do, without knowing it, whatever is necessary to preserve it—the parts are adapted to the requirements of the whole. But this reverses the picture we were given earlier. It is now impossible to "start" from the (socially embedded) individual and "build up" the social order that emerges undesigned from his choices. On the contrary, we have to know about the social order, the traditions that constitute it, and the systems of rules of individual conduct, to make sense of the actions of the individual agents:

> the order which will form as the result of these actions is of course in no sense "part of the purpose" or of the motive of the acting individuals. The immediate cause, the impulse which drives them to act, will be something affecting them only . . . while this consequence . . . is wholly beyond their knowledge or intentions. (Hayek, 1967: 77)

The social scientist therefore has to keep in mind *two rationalities*—the "immediate cause" of action, which concerns only the actor, and the ultimate or "final" cause or purpose, the maintenance of the social system. Neither makes sense without the other. We are now applying the intentional stance at a collective level, just as Dennett himself does:

> There is no substitute for the intentional stance. Either you adopt it, and explain the pattern by finding the semantic-level facts, or you will forever be baffled by the regularity—the *causal* regularity—that is manifestly there. . . . Even if you can describe, in matchless microdetail, every causal fact in the history of every giraffe who has ever lived, unless you go up a level or two and ask "Why?" . . . you will never be able to *explain* the manifest regularities, such as the fact that giraffes have come to have long necks. (1995: 421)

So we are presented with syntactic-level facts, facts about the rules determining the microlevel choices of the individual agent, and semantic-level facts, facts about their *meaning*, their function for the social order. To explain the manifest regularities—the instances of social coordination and discoordination—we cannot confine ourselves to the former. We cannot start with the microlevel choices of the individual agent and build up, because we are failing to ask "Why?" Not why the individual does what he does—that is in response to his incentives: We can all agree on the immediate cause. But why the incentives guide the individual to *this* outcome rather than *that*—what is the purpose, or "final cause." The system of incentives facing the individual fulfill that purpose because *this* is functional for the social entity within which the individual is operating—but that can never be understood by applying *Verstehen* to the behavior of the individual.

In his discussion of social evolution, Hayek invokes the intentional stance at a collective level—he asks what is necessary to serve a rationality at a higher level than that of the individual human being: "Frequently the behaviour of the individual is determined by his success in maintaining himself as part of a certain system within which it is . . . the whole system to which he has adapted that determines his behaviour. For this reason, value . . . can only be understood as the determinant of what people must do to maintain the overall structure" (1983: 36). So, for Hayek, the individual has to adapt to the rationality of the system, and it is the system that determines the behavior of the individual. What we think of as *value* is just a signal to us to act in accordance with the needs of the higher rationality of the system. To try to exclude this, to build an account purely in terms of the rationality of the individual, would be to "confine ourselves to less than we know about the situation." In his work on the evolution of social orders, Hayek thus abandons the individualist methodology he had proposed in his wartime writings, thereby rectifying the inconsistency that that precept implied for the system of his thought.

In moving away from what he wrote in the 1940s, Hayek is also moving farther away from the founders of the Austrian school. This cannot be dealt with fully here, and forms the subject of further research. Nevertheless, as a footnote to what has gone before, we may compare Hayek's stance here with that of Mises in *Human Action* (Mises, 1996). Under the rubric of "The Principle of Methodological Individualism," Mises explains that "Praxeology deals with the actions of individual men. It is only in the further course of its inquiries that cognition of human cooperation is attained and social action is treated as a special case of the more universal category of human action as such" (Mises, 1996: 41). For Mises, "social action" is clearly to be subsumed under individual action, as a special case of the latter. As will be apparent from the discussion above, this is wholly at odds with Hayek's approach, according to which individual actions can only be understood once we understand the social entities for which those actions are functional. We should note that even Hayek's initial standpoint diverges from Mises here: Even when Hayek held that social science should start with individuals and build up, the individual was conceived as a node embedded in a nexus of social relations, but there is no hint of such an insight in Mises's account. Collective wholes or social entities do indeed exist for Mises, but they *can* be understood, and indeed *only* be understood, via the individual actions that they consist of: "If we scrutinize the meaning of the various actions performed by individuals we must necessarily learn everything about the actions of collective wholes . . . the way to a cognition of collective wholes is through an analysis of the individuals' actions" (Mises, 1996: 42). The notion that social entities have their own logic is utterly foreign to this standpoint. Whereas for Hayek, standing on the shoulders of Adam Smith and Adam Ferguson, the focus of social science is always the unintended outcomes of purposive behavior. It is remarkable, indeed diagnostic, that in the 900-odd pages of *Human Action* there is but one reference to unintended outcomes—and that one occasion is an explanation that a specific social phenomenon is *not* an unintended outcome of intentional behavior (Mises, 1996: 449).

CONCLUSION

This chapter has considered the methodological stance that Hayek prescribed in his wartime writings, identifying what within it can and cannot be sustained. While much there was found to be commendable, his specifically individualist methodological prescription was found to be questionable. The chapter suggests that in his later writings on evolution he shifts away from the methodologically individualist precepts expressed in the earlier work. A particular issue of interest uniting the narrative has been the focus on Dennett's *intentional stance*. It was argued that Hayek's earlier writings expressed and indeed were enriched by the adoption of this standpoint. Moreover, the article suggests that Hayek's later writings, on the topic of the evolution of social institutions, continued to apply the intentional stance, but by extending its field of application beyond that of the individual human actor, broke with his earlier and more limited views. This article has not made any attempt to appraise Hayek's evolutionary theory, a topic that is addressed in Andy Denis (2002). The extent to which Hayek's view can be taken as representing the Austrian school—its consistency or otherwise with, for example, the views of Carl Menger and Ludwig von Mises—is not addressed here and constitutes the topic of further work in this area, although I strongly suspect that Hayek is in many respects something of an outlier within the Austrian school, so far as these issues are concerned.

REFERENCES

Denis, Andy. 2002. "Was Hayek a Panglossian Evolutionary Theorist? A Reply to Whitman." *Constitutional Political Economy*, 13(3): 275–285.

Dennett, Daniel C. 1996. *The Intentional Stance*. Cambridge, MA: The MIT Press.

———. 1995. *Darwin's Dangerous Idea: Evolution and the Meanings of Life.* London: Penguin.
Hayek, F. A. 1983. *Knowledge, Evolution and Society.* London: Adam Smith Institute.
———. 1979. *The Counter-Revolution of Science*, 2nd ed. Indianapolis: Liberty Press.
———. 1967. *Studies in Philosophy, Politics and Economics.* London: Routledge & Kegan Paul.
———. 1952. *The Sensory Order: An Inquiry into the Foundations of Theoretical Psychology*. London: Routledge & Kegan Paul.
———. 1944. "Scientism and the Study of Society. Part III." *Economica* New Series, 11 (41), Feb: 27–39.
———. 1943. "Scientism and the Study of Society. Part II." *Economica* New Series, 10 (37), Feb: 34–63.
———. 1942. "Scientism and the Study of Society. Part I." *Economica* New Series, 9 (35) (August): 267–291.
Marx, Karl. 1973. *Grundrisse: Foundations of the Critique of Political Economy (Rough Draft)*. Harmondsworth: Penguin for *New Left Review.*
Mises, Ludwig von. (1996) *Human Action.* 4th ed. San Francisco: Fox & Wilkes.

CHAPTER 2

From Methodological Individualism to Emergence, Ecology, and the Fluid Self: Exploring the Shift from Misesian to Hayekian Social Science*

Gus diZerega

Entering a new intellectual watershed can be as subtle as entering a new natural one. In the latter case, initially the trees and shrubs are the same, as are the animals. The climate has not changed, and even the scenery is familiar. But over time and distance an entirely new ecology often presents itself.

I contend this happened in the Austrian School in the shift many made from a focus on Ludwig von Mises' praxeology to F. A. Hayek's emphasis on spontaneous orders and market processes.

What both approaches shared, the common slope dividing these two watersheds so to speak, was a joint appreciation for how the market price system coordinated the use of resources more efficiently than could any

*I am grateful to Andy Denis and Guinevere Nell, two additional authors in this collection, for their generous feedback on an earlier version of this chapter. While dealing with their insights enriched this chapter, its arguments are ultimately my own responsibility.

alternative. In addition, each economist contributed powerfully to developing a devastating critique of arguments that economies could be centrally planned. Mises pioneered this argument, and Hayek developed it further while responding to socialists' efforts at rebutting Mises (Mises, 2011; Hayek, 1948).

And yet, despite these similarities and despite Hayek's having been Mises' student, their intellectual worlds increasingly diverged, although neither chose to discuss the issue (Caldwell, 2004: 144–144, 148).

Mises was the strictest of methodological individualists. His "praxeology" sought to develop an "apodictically certain" science of human action based on the fact every individual acts purposefully. Ultimately the logic of acting individuals, plus history, was the foundation for genuine knowledge of human society. Mises created an abstract logical model into which anyone could fit any empirical example, and the model would cover it. (2007)

Hayek had never accepted Mises' view of an a priori praxeology as the best foundation for the social sciences, and throughout his career he moved steadily away from any form of methodological individualism (Caldwell, 2004: 419–422). Alan Denis (this volume) explores this issue in-depth in the present volume. Hayek ultimately focused on markets as discovery and coordination processes without either a clear beginning or end. This is an ecological or evolutionary perspective. Hayek ultimately described the market itself as a spontaneous order, a complex adaptive system shaping distributed knowledge known to no one in its entirety, through an ongoing process of discovery aided by prices arising out of previous actions of the same sort. Not only could such an order not be deliberately created by central direction, a point on which he and Mises agreed, but it could not be understood simply through unpacking the logic of human action.

For Hayek, even individual rationality grew out of patterns of social cooperation that arose for quite different purposes and required no human rationality to do so. In volume 3 of *Law, Legislation and Liberty*, he wrote,

> It is . . . misleading to represent the individual brain or mind as the capping stone of the hierarchy of complex structures produced by evolution. . . . The mind is embedded in a traditional impersonal structure of learnt rules, and its capacity to order experience is an acquired replica of a cultural pattern which every individual mind finds given. . . . [M]ind can exist only as part of another independently existing distinct structure or order, though that order persists and can develop only because millions of minds constantly absorb and modify parts of it. (1979: 157)

Oddly, Mises seemed to agree at least abstractly, but did not follow through on the implications (Nell, this volume). One could not begin with individual action in any philosophically or methodologically reductionist sense because the individual was already a product of such systems.

For Mises, prices were signals for individuals, providing information they needed to achieve their goals more effectively. The better the price system worked, the more closely the market could approach a perfect coordination of human plans without anyone's intending it. Hayek did not deny this important dimension existed, but regarded the market as an ongoing process in which *disequilibrating* factors were as important as equilibrating ones. Moreover, the market was but one spontaneous order among many. Hayek referred to science, custom, and language as "others." We were as much products of these processes as they were products of our choices.

Borders and boundaries sharply defined within Misesian reductionism became blurry and continually interpenetrated one another within Hayek's approach. Nowhere was this more important than in the concept of the individual. As I will show, subsequent work in a variety of fields far removed from economics has increased the significance of this change in perspective. The individual by no means disappears, but takes on a very different character from how it has usually been conceived in Western social science.

RETHINKING INDIVIDUALISM

In some important sense we are unique individuals. But we are also beings crucially shaped by time, place, and many key experiences of our lives, often experiences over which we have no control. These create psychological and behavioral patterns common to many rather than unique to any. Yet individuality is a universal of human experience. How do these contrasting insights fit together? I think sociologists Peter Berger and Thomas Luckmann gave an exceptionally good start to answering these questions, a start in keeping with Hayekian insights.

Berger and Luckmann contended understanding individuals required us to keep three perspectives *simultaneously* in mind. They argue, "Society is a human product. Society is an objective reality. Man is a social product. An analysis that leaves out any one of these three moments will be distortive. Only with the transmission of the social world to a new generation (that is, internalization as effectuated by socialization) does the fundamental social dialectic appear in its totality" (1967: 61).

Let us unpack what they meant.

1. *Society is created by the actions of individuals*. This insight captures the core of methodological individualism, and as far as it goes, is important and true. Both praxeology and the dominant contemporary alternative of rational choice theory stop here. But by itself

this principle is not able to carry the causal weight such theorists pile upon it. Two other principles apply equally.

2. *Individuals are social creations.* We deeply reflect our place and time. We think with concepts we inherit and only slightly modify, always within a larger context we have no choice but to take for granted. Albert Einstein could never have arisen on the Lakota Reservation in South Dakota, nor could Lakota medicine person Black Elk have become the man he was in late nineteenth-century central Europe. Had they been switched at birth, they would have become *different people.* As Émile Durkheim's pioneering study showed, even so intensely personal behavior as suicide varies in frequency from society to society (1997). All our characteristics, from our language and customs to our most personal psychology, bear the imprint of our culture. Hayek's observation that we learn to act rationally from living in social groups is one important example of this principle.
3. *Society is encountered by individuals as an objective reality.* We are born knowing nothing or next to nothing about our world. Newborns become members of their society by learning how members of that society make sense of things, and adopting this model for themselves. Initially they are not aware of alternative perspectives. They do not so much choose as absorb what they do not yet have the capacity to question. What constitutes a mother or a father is accepted as uncritically as what constitutes a rock or tree.

Even later in life we exist within social networks that powerfully shape who we are and what we are likely to think. Recent research in psychology reveals that depression appears to be contagious (Haeffel and Hames, 2013; Cacioppo et al., 2009). These networks also appear to influence our other emotions and even our physical health (Christakis and Fowler, 2009). Nicholas Christakis and James Fowler concluded from their studies of social networks that "Happiness, in short, is not merely a function of personal experience, but also is a property of groups. Emotions are a collective phenomenon" (2008). This shaping goes beyond emotions. In the *New Scientist*, Alex Pentland concluded that "most of our public beliefs are learned by observing the attitudes, actions, and outcomes of peers rather than by logic or argument" (2014: 31).

In other words, a great deal of what we do does not arise from deliberately choosing among alternatives, and is profoundly shaped by social contexts. For example, fluent speakers of a language rarely search for "the right word" even when saying something they have never said before. Many of our choices in life are made on the surface of a deep sea of knowledge, most of which is tacit unless something arises to bring it to the surface and make us aware of it (Polanyi, 1958; Noë, 2009). Speech is certainly one such instance. In addition, our choices often do not involve a sharp distinction between ends and means, unlike Mises' praxeological assumptions. Again speech is often an example.

Customs and beliefs are experienced as so real that many people have great difficulty imagining life could succeed with different customs and beliefs. Learning that there are different ways of living that work for others is one of the great enriching and often transformative experiences of travel to foreign lands.

But we are not simple products of our social relations.

While beginning in infancy the child encounters a socially mediated reality it accepts as simply the way things are, to some degree it eventually can question *parts* of what it once took for granted. This begins when the child believes that two messages it receives do not fit together, and so separates itself to some degree from both in order to evaluate this apparent contradiction. This process continues into adulthood. And so we return to individual action, that first "moment."

But no matter how creative we might be, we cannot stand outside *all* of our socially acquired knowledge and evaluate it. No matter how sophisticated our questions, we always ask them within a social context that must remain largely taken for granted. Réne Descartes thought he had penetrated as far as one could go when he concluded "I think therefore I am." A Buddhist scholar of the time would have had a very different take on his insight.

METHODOLOGICAL INDIVIDUALISM

Methodological individualism makes no claims about how our intentions arise. As a method, it is as compatible with the work of Jürgen Habermas as it is with rational choice theory (Stanford Encyclopedia, 2010: 11). Methodological individualism's central claim is that action-theoretic levels of explanation in the social sciences enable us to understand social phenomena in a way inaccessible to the natural sciences. Actions are motivated by intentions, and we can understand them as such, even when the actual result of these actions is unintended and even undesired by the actor. Its explanatory power arises from its capacity to show how unexpected consequences arise from action intended to accomplish very different goals, as when rent controls lead to *reduced* populations in Berkeley (diZerega, 2000: 311–314).

Berger and Luckmann certainly thought their model was compatible with methodological individualism. Here Paul Lewis shed additional light on this issue, demonstrating they had gone beyond a strictly methodological individualist approach. Lewis writes, "While in his explicit comments Berger eschews emergent social properties and portrays social structure as being ontologically reducible to human agency, his substantive work presupposes that social structures are ontologically irreducible to human agency, not least because such structures are the bearers of emergent causal powers" (2010: 212).

Berger and Luckmann's model does not exist in any linear sense, starting with the individual acting and building from there because *the three "moments" are always simultaneous,* creating an enduring and dynamic pattern of relationships out of which both individuals and societies *emerge.* Society cannot exist without individual understandings, but individual understandings cannot exist without society, and many of those understandings are not the product of a choice. As the African proverb puts it, "I am because we are."

While methodological individualism argues that purposes cannot exist without purposive actors, actors always act in networks and systems existing independently from them, while shaping their perceptions and choices. These systems possess their own dynamics involving rules with biases of which no actor need be aware. For example, as a complex adaptive system, the market strengthens certain values independently from the intentions of individuals acting within them (diZerega, 1997). Most of these structures invisibly shape what people see as the opportunities they confront. As they do, all else being equal, people whose values are more in harmony with those privileged by these systems will do better in systems terms than will people with different value hierarchies. For example, the values that make for a good businessman and the values that make for a good scientist are not the same. Many people do well in one such system and not in the other.

Methodological individualism is not so much wrong as it is so incomplete as to be misleading. It works well enough when contexts of choice do not matter and values are purely instrumental, but much of the time this is not the case (Nell, this volume). As Lewis saw, Berger and Luckmann had crossed into another intellectual watershed. Without noticing it, they had entered the same watershed as had Hayek.

Blurred Boundaries

Methodological individualism treats the individual actor as importantly distinct from both its environment and even its body *at the time of acting.* We see the latter exemplified in the argument by many libertarians that the individual "owns" his or her body. Being "owned," the body becomes an object whose value is rooted in the preferences of its ghostly owner. The same logic applies to owning a car or a pencil.

This outlook appears intuitive to people who have grown up within a Christian, and particularly a Protestant Christian, culture. As we are alone before God, we are alone before others and isolated within our world. Traditional Western models of individuals emphasize their distinctiveness from their contexts. Our dominant religions and customs reinforce this way of viewing ourselves. From Christianity to John Locke to Descartes to Jean-Paul Sartre to Ayn Rand, we are considered as distinct from our environment. This prereflective foundation to understanding our being in the world is learned while we are very young. It is not chosen, and is initially accepted uncritically. This foundational status in our culture explains its power, which is much greater than the arguments its adherents can field on its behalf. I think this cultural bias helps explain the continuing attraction of methodological individualist ways of thinking despite the arguments of scholars such as Hayek, Berger, and Luckmann.

Today this cultural bias is now being undermined from another direction. As it is, the power of Hayek's arguments and the persuasiveness of the model that Berger and Luckmann developed is strengthened. To skip ahead, this new perspective not so much rejects methodological individualist insights as situates them within a larger context of emergent processes. Doing so profoundly alters what we think of as individuals, even at the purely mental level of the individual who makes decisions and then acts on them.

Once scientists became capable of examining organisms' genomes, unexpected discoveries arose challenging characteristics we traditionally thought defined individuals. Long thought to be analytically distinguishable from their environment and from other organisms, individuals have been found to have blurred boundaries at every level and in every dimension, from mental to all levels of the biological. Along the way, venerable distinctions in the social and natural sciences, such as "nature versus nurture" have been found to be flawed formulations. This new perspective is an ecological or evolutionary one, and it holds "all the way down."

Eukaryotic Cells

Eukaryotic comprise us and all other life other than bacteria and archaea. They differ from prokaryotic cells in organisms like bacteria and archaea in having a nucleus. They also have organelles such as mitochondria, and in plants, chloroplasts, whereas bacteria and archaea generally lack these structures.

These intracellular bodies' DNA is different from the DNA in the cell's nucleus. They are, or at least were, distinct organisms. The best present guess as to how eukaryotic cells originated is that one bacteria engulfed another and instead of absorbing it, entered into a symbiotic relationship with it. Alternatively, perhaps the smaller organism that is now an organelle invaded the larger as a parasite, and over time developed a symbiotic and finally fused relationship with its one-time host. Over time, the two became inseparable. Symbiosis became unity. Whatever the cause, all subsequent development of complex life depends on this extraordinary foundation. The theory developing this insight is called endosymbiosis (Margulis, 1970).

If the cells that constitute all complex life exist due to symbiotic rather than competitive relationships, symbiosis is at least as fundamental as competition in evolution, and arguably more so. The weighing of outcomes to privilege cooperation over competition seems to be inherent in the logic of relationships (Axelrod, 2006). But this discovery was only the tip of an amazing iceberg.

VIRUSES

A single eukaryotic cell, such as an amoeba, is still very far from a multicellular organism. The latter requires cell fusion proteins to enable cells to form tissues rather than exist independently. So far, all the cell fusion proteins that have been discovered originated in viruses and later appeared in eukaryotic cells. Because not all such proteins have yet been analyzed, the research is not yet decisive. But based on what is now known, it was viruses infecting eukaryotic cells that modified their internal structures, enabling them to band together to form muscles and other tissues. If this research holds up, entities so simple that they arguably are not even alive are responsible for all complex multicellular life (Slezak, 2014: 16).

BACTERIA

Our bodies contain about ten microbial cells for every genetically human one, and about 400 microbial genes for every human one. The interrelationships between the human body and the bacteria inhabiting it are often so mutually beneficial, that our long taken-for-granted concept of a human organism needs to be reconsidered. Some biologists argue it is more accurate to describe us as meta- or superorganisms (Milius, 2014: 15). Twenty-six leading scientists in this field of research argued in the *Proceedings of the National Academy of Science* that the animal-bacteria relationship can most appropriately be described as an ecosystem (McFall-Ngai, 2013).

For example, newborn mammals acquire important bacteria during their birth passage through the vagina. In experiments with mice, as mother mice were stressed, the bacterial content within their vaginas changed. Their pups picked up different bacteria, ones associated with stress that became the dominant bacteria in their gut.

Significantly, the brains of pups born to stressed mothers developed differently from the brains of mice born to unstressed mothers (*New Scientist*, 11/23/2013: 18). Their gut bacterial population appears to be a crucial element in these different outcomes. The population of beneficial bacteria is reduced in the former, and their absence ultimately distorts the further development of their brains (Sanders, 12/14/13: 13).

In addition, in breast milk many sugars nourish bacteria rather than infants. Far from being nutritional thieves, these bacteria play an important role in shaping the infant's immune system. They help beneficial bacteria colonize the gut, triggering genes that help protect babies from pathogens (Shugart, 2014: 22).

Bacteria may also play an important role in how evolutionary processes unfold in the world. Certain bacteria have been found to be essential for some insect species to form viable eggs. Others determine whether cross-species breeding is viable, and so their absence might play an important role in speciation. They even significantly influence the selection of mates (Saey, 2013: 19; Milius, 2014: 17).

Meta-organism, superorganism, or ecosystem, we are far from the traditional idea of what constitutes a physical individual. Groups are the units of selection rather than traditional individuals at any level. In discussing group selection in biology and in Hayek's work, Todd Zwicki writes, "If groups of genes can work together as single individuals . . . why can't groups of individuals similarly work together as single groups?" (2000: 85; Sober and Wilson 1998: 88).

Interestingly, in mainstream biology the idea of meta- or superorganisms is winning renewed interest in other areas. In his most recent work, E. O. Wilson (2012) has rejected the "selfish gene" hypothesis that he and Richard Dawkins made so dominant in NeoDarwinian theory. He was led to this step by his ongoing research into social insects. Wilson now argues for group selection, with the groups being superorganisms, such as ant colonies. Wilson and his supporters in biology lend important support to Hayek's (1988) argument for group selection in human society.

Given the discoveries regarding the role of bacteria in the functioning of individuals subject to evolutionary pressures, the dividing line between groups and individuals has become very fine indeed.

It gets finer still.

CHIMERAS

The term for having more than a single genome active within an organism is "chimera." Our genome was long thought to be uniquely our own. No longer. As the cost of DNA examination has fallen, what was once thought a very rare condition in which a human being possessed more than a single genome has turned out to be common. For example, a woman needing a kidney transplant was tested to enable her to find a match. The results were entirely unexpected. Describing this incident, Carl Zimmer wrote tests "indicated that she was not the mother of two of her three biological children. It turned out that she had originated from two genomes. One genome gave rise to her blood and some of her eggs; other eggs carried a separate genome" (2013).

Many mothers have cells from their fetus living in different parts of their bodies, including the lung, thyroid muscle, liver, heart, kidney, skin, and even the brain. Robert Martone wrote in *Scientific American*, "These may have a broad range of impacts, from tissue repair and cancer prevention to sparking immune disorders." There is evidence that women with such cells in their brain are less likely to acquire Alzheimer's (Martone, 2012; Chan, et al. 2012).

Many of us are chimeras, blurring the distinction between our organism and another. Nor are biological and mental boundaries only blurred within what we long considered our bodies as contrasted to others' bodies. This blurring extends beyond our bodies as well.

EPIGENETICS

Since Lanark's theories failed to shed light on adaptive processes that Darwin correctly identified, and particularly since the rise of NeoDarwinism, which integrated his work with genetics, evolutionary adaptation was thought to take place solely through chance mutations of the genome. Nature edited out disadvantageous changes and so selected for more advantageous ones. This simple model has now been abandoned for one that sees a more dynamic relationship between organisms and their environment.

Environmental conditions and even social interactions can modify the genome's expression, not only in the organism directly experiencing the influence but also in future generations. This happens even though the genome is unaltered. Epigenetics explores this newly discovered fact.

Cell DNA requires additional information to tell the DNA what genes to transcribe. Environmental influences can influence DNA, leading to activation of different sets of genes. Epigenetics thus accounts for something long thought impossible: "post natal inheritance," in which even though no changes in the genetic code have occurred, heritable traits arise to influence future generations.

Both physical and psychological influences can trigger epigenetic phenomena.

In one important experiment, the offspring of bullied male mice were prevented from meeting their fathers. They nevertheless grew up hypersensitive to stress. Neuroscientist Eric Nestler said, "It was not a subtle effect; the offspring were dramatically more susceptible to developing signs of depression" (Hurley, 2013). The mechanics of this process are not yet understood, for if females were artificially inseminated with the sperm of bullied males, the effect was weaker.

Even so, memory has been proven to some degree heritable because of another experiment. Male mice were trained to associate the smell of orange blossoms with receiving a shock. Their sperm was then used in in vitro fertilization. Their children *and their grandchildren* were startled when encountering the smell of orange blossoms for the first time. This was not the case with mice whose parents (or grandparents) had not been so conditioned (Sanders, 12/1/13; Dias and Ressler, 2014).

NATURE

Apparently chemicals in the environment can also produce epigenetic changes in organisms that last generations. The offspring of rats exposed to Vinclozolin, a fungicide still used in the United States, demonstrated not only more sensitivity to stress, but they were less interested in new environments and individuals than normal rats. These changes were still noticeable among the *grandchildren* of exposed rats. Michael Skinner explained, "The ancestral exposure of your great grandmother alters your brain development to then respond to stress differently." He added that before these experiments, researchers "did not know a stress response could be programmed by your ancestors' environmental exposures" (Agence France-Presse, 2012).

The dominant American view of individuals is deeply undermined by findings such as these. I suspect a large part of the hostility directed toward Rachel Carson's *Silent Spring* (1962) stemmed not simply from the financial interests of chemical companies, but it also was rooted in the book's undermining of the belief that individuals are ultimately completely separate entities from one another and from the world. Compared to what we now know, Carson had only scratched the surface.

Not all environmental influences are negative. Exposure to specific bacteria in the soil demonstrably reduces anxiety in mice by influencing the serotonin levels in their brains. But this was not all it did. Researchers discovered mice fed these bacteria "navigated [a] maze twice as fast and with less demonstrated anxiety [than did] control mice." These effects declined once the bacteria were no longer present within the mice. While still faster than the controls, after three weeks their performance was no longer statistically significant (*Science Daily*, 2010).

People breathe or ingest these bacteria when spending time out of doors, particularly when in close contact with the soil. Bacteria that normally live externally to mice, and presumably ourselves, can alter the mood and increase the intelligence of mice, and perhaps ourselves as well. So much for separating mind from nature.

Our connections with the outside world go even farther. In "A Dose of Nature," Jules Pretty and Jo Barton found people's mood and self-esteem benefited from what they call "green exercise" (2010). Pretty explained, "For the first time in the scientific literature, we have been able to show dose-response relationships for the positive effects of nature on human mental health" (2010).

Their findings applied to all ages and both genders, although there were interesting differences among them. The biggest benefits applied to the mentally ill. Reporting on this research, Peter Stanford wrote,

> being in a green environment is better than being in an urban one in terms of a measurable positive effect on blood pressure, hormones and stress levels. Intriguingly, it also concludes that the biggest beneficial boost from exposure to nature is gained within the initial five minutes of each encounter with the great outdoors. While it continues to reap a harvest thereafter, the crop of positives diminishes. (2010)

Perhaps even more unexpectedly, living in more complex natural environments has measurably better mental health impacts than living in simpler ones, and both are superior to being surrounded by concrete and traffic. Better mental health is encouraged by the presence of biodiversity (Herro, 2007; Dobbs, 2007).

We experience our life as a unified consciousness; we have an "I," a strong sense of "self." But the physical dimensions of our bodies include separate organisms all the way down to the intra-cellular level. Nor are they distinct from our minds. These different organisms apparently impact our intelligence and emotions alike. Yet our awareness of ourselves as a distinct organism is fundamental to who we are and how we live our lives. Individuals definitely exist. I am one and so are you. But we need to think about individuals, including ourselves, differently.

EMERGENCE

Individuals are *emergent phenomena* nested within an extraordinarily complex web of relationships from the intracellular level up to the wider physical environment. Similarly, our social environment shapes our psychological and physical well-being. At a physical level our self-awareness appears to emerge from the interaction of many different parts of our brain rather than being the product of a specific part of it (Lewis, 2012). Our subjective experience of self-awareness is also quite variable and connected to the context of our experience. Probably all of us have experienced sudden pain such as a stubbed toe or smashed thumb, where our world suddenly diminishes to a single point of agony. At other times it expands to include others, as when we open our hearts to a loved one or empathetically identify with a person crippled by disease. We now find we have a similar variability physically.

Emergence refers to phenomena that arise from and are not reducible to the qualities of their parts. Instead, the pattern of *relationships* into which the parts enter brings forth new phenomena, be they physical or mental. In his discussion of Berger and Luckmann, Paul Lewis offered a clear description of what constitute emergent phenomena.

> *emergence* refers to the possibility that, when certain elements or parts stand in particular relations to one another, the whole that is formed has properties (including causal powers, defined as the capacity to behave in a particular way and to bring about effects of a particular kind) that are not possessed by its constituent elements taken in isolation. The properties that arise when the elements are arranged in the requisite way are known as emergent properties, while any whole that possesses an emergent property is known as an emergent or 'higher-level' entity. (2010)

Hayek's theory of the market as a discovery process generating predictable patterns is an example of emergent phenomena. So are the other spontaneous orders of science, democracy, and the World Wide Web (diZerega, 2013).

Human awareness and society are both emergent. Berger and Luckmann's discussion demonstrates how our individuality emerges from our immersion in social relations that are themselves products of human action. Neither reduces to the other, but both emerge and change from out of the network of relationships comprising human existence. This process is what Joanna Macy (1991) calls "mutual causality."

Biology now indicates human organisms are emergent in every way, taking their mental *and* physical attributes from immersion within an external social and natural ecology and from their internal ecology. We are who we are because of symbiotic internal relationships with viruses and bacteria, as well as external relationships within a larger interpenetrating environment. These relationships are not just physical. If the experiments with mice apply to mammals in general, even our intelligence is an emergent quality connected with nature, not just because it emerged from evolutionary processes but also because it is sustained by ecological ones. Of course boundaries exist, but they are not rigid or complete, and their permeability is partly why they work for us.

If emergent systems shape our minds and are not simply neutral media for transmitting choices, methodological individualism is not only incomplete, it is incapable of identifying the core nature and consequences of *human* action. As Berger and Luckmann observed, it is distortive.

If this research I have described is accurate, the core of our individuality is not nature and not nurture. We are not born with an irreducible character, but neither is it our unique physical characteristics nor our specific social context; rather, *it is the creative unity emerging from out of our experience as a human being.* It is a unity we to some degree consciously create, *but only to some degree.* An individual is a creative accomplishment, and to some degree we are co-creators of ourselves.

Human individuality is a process and manifestation of creative discovery, bringing forth a world that would otherwise not exist. And worlds are created out of relationships. To me this fact provides a far better foundation for appreciating the moral value of individuals than their having rights bestowed on them by some deity or philosopher, or being regarded as valuable in their equality rather than in their individuality. The evolutionary/ecological turn that Hayek helped begin and that Berger and Luckmann did much to clarify at an abstract level is working itself out in extraordinarily profound and unexpected ways.

The Elusive Self and "Self-Interest"

As a society we are shifting from viewing our world as one of discrete objects engaged in external relations with one another to one of interpenetrating relationships bringing forth qualities possessed by none of their components either individually or collectively. During much of the past century, scientists explored these phenomena in physics. The same thing was happening in the science of ecology. Toward the century's end, the discovery of endosymbiosis expanded this outlook into biology. During the past few years, this process has further transformed the biological and mental world, so that today our bodies can be reasonably described as ecosystems and our consciousness as importantly shaped and perhaps created by this ecosystem. Human individuals are expressions not only of the relationships comprising the ecosystem that is our body, but we also reflect our relationships within the eco- and social systems outside our body.

Modernity's transformations are also largely emergent phenomena arising from people's entering into progressively more specialized cooperative relationships. Science, the market, democracy, and the World Wide Web are examples. They are creating an increasingly rich social ecosystem, one more resembling a lush rainforest than an arctic tundra. Such ecosystems generate increasing richness and diversity among their inhabitants, who in turn help sustain it.

Economic theory is one field in which this transformation in our understanding might have profound implications. The usual economic model, including Austrian theory, views the market as a competitive process generated by self-interested individuals. But those individuals have *variable* selves. They vary depending on *which* self is engaged in viewing its place in the world. If soon after I bash my thumb I see a legless person in a wheelchair, my relevant self and its perceived interests will often change dramatically. *Both selves and interests make sense only within contexts, and relevant contexts are not fixed.*

My self is a unity built out of relationships, but beyond simple awareness, every specific element of that unity is able to shift and change, and as it does, my "self" changes. In this sense the self is complex. Such a self is a creative achievement in harmonizing many of the dimensions that go into who we are while engaging in projects. Since what constitutes "self-interest" emerges from out of my relationships, and those are variable, *there is no stable or certain self-interest.* It varies with the perspective I take, and that perspective varies depending on the context to which I am attending, apparently including elements of which I am consciously unaware. This rather strange way of putting it is a logical outgrowth of realizing that the self does not exist independently of its relationships. It also shifts our focus on the nature of economic action.

This model is also fundamentally cooperative rather than competitive. Market competition grows out of cooperation in circumstances where information is incomplete. Every market transaction begins cooperatively, from creating a business to buying a product. Competition arises when people acting on incompatible plans seek resources. Even if I want to go into competition with someone, I must first create a cooperative set of relationships so as to bring my product or service to people's attention.

Lynn Margulis, the biologist who did so much to direct scientific attention to symbiosis, argues that NeoDarwinian evolutionary theory gave far too much emphasis to interorganismic competition. She contended history would ultimately judge this emphasis as "a minor twentieth-century religious sect within the sprawling religious persuasion of Anglo-Saxon Biology" (Mann, 1991). The same may ultimately be judged true for economics and competition, and for largely the same reasons. Symbiosis is too little examined in modern economics as it was long too little examined in modern NeoDarwinism. My chapter in this book's companion volume begins to explore this argument (2014).

Relationships can change, and if they generate emergent phenomena, as they change new emergent patterns can appear. Traditional analyses focusing only on individuals have a hard time handling many of these social phenomena, and sometimes lead us into absurdity.

COMPREHENDING FREEDOM

Nell (this volume) explores the importance of the concept of the public good in a world of what I would call complex selves. Individualist approaches have great trouble with the concept. In a telling example, George Mason University's (GMU's) Mercatus Center recently identified California and New York as the "least free" states in the union, whereas states like North Dakota followed by Oklahoma, South Dakota, Tennessee, and New Hampshire were the "freest" (2013). But in response to this report, very few (if any) "freedom lovers" sought to move from California or New York to these havens of liberty.

The reason for the disjunction between the actions of those claiming to love freedom and their explicit definition of it is that their explicit understanding is inferior to the tacit knowledge of freedom. Theirs is an example of what Hayek called the errors of constructivism: the view that we have sufficient knowledge to rebuild society according to a blueprint, in this case a libertarian one. This is an instance of constructivism or rationalism (Callahan, 2013).

Freedom arises from our relationships. How could it not, since we ourselves arise from our relationships? And not from just any relationship, but from those that enlarge the meaningful choices open to us. Freedom is voluntary, but it is not just voluntary. *Freedom must involve all three Bergerian "moments" to be fully understood.*

Robinson Crusoe alone on his island was as free from human coercion as a man could be. In terms of negative liberty, no one was freer. In addition, he had plenty of food, shelter, and leisure. Even so, Crusoe wanted to be rescued, and not because he found his "freedom" intolerable. The sphere of enriching *relationships* into which people can enter is much larger in Bismarck, North Dakota, than on Crusoe's island, and Crusoe would feel *and be* freer there. But in that sense San Francisco, Los Angeles, and New York beat both.

To pick an economic example, California is number one in high-tech start-ups and New York is number two. California's rank is falling, and government might play a role here, but the state catching up with it is New York! None of the states judged most "free" are even on the map (Ouimet, 2012). In addition, property values in New York and California are much higher than in the "freest" states, yet according to free market theory, the real estate market reflects people's variable demand to live somewhere. Why are rational freedom-loving individuals not seeking to move from California and New York to North Dakota, South Dakota, Oklahoma, Tennessee, and New Hampshire, thereby driving up property values and reducing them in New York and California?

A purely individualist approach to understanding human beings ended up with an absurd conclusion *the theorists themselves do not honor.*

Here is a key to how methodological individualism distorts our understanding of important social phenomena. Isolated from any context, regulations impose limits on what the regulated can do, and so limit their freedom. Considered from the standpoint of the isolated individual, limitations on choices due to government bans and regulations narrow the variety of mutually beneficial transactions into which individuals can enter. Government is a *limitation* on freedom. Therefore, states with the fewest regulations are freer than states that have them. This is a natural deduction from those using the most abstract kinds of methodologically individualist analyses, such as Murray Rothbard (1970).

As to explaining the apparent preference of most people for less "freedom" over more, a reader of an earlier version of this paper wrote George Mason University scholars "point to the spontaneous order of the market, in which greater network connections produce greater economic growth" and "people prefer income to freedom . . . even though greater freedom in the cities would lead to higher growth . . ." There are two levels of error here. The first is a failure to understand human existence at a very basic level, and the second has to do with not understanding emergent orders such as the market.

Jane Jacobs' *The Death and Life of Great American Cities* was the first book to treat cities as complex emergent social ecosystems (1961). Since its publication, her findings have been shown to be well taken (Scott, 1998). Cities develop qualities that cannot be reduced to individual interactions. For example, they require proportionately less infrastructure as (1) population increases, and as there are increases in (2) the production of wealth, whether defined as GDP, income, or wages; crime; and (3) "markers of innovation" such as numbers of patents filed or people engaged in creative careers in science and the arts (Ehrenberg, 2013: 5). The first could be called an economy of scale, but the others are not.

Luis Bettencourt of the Santa Fe Institute writes, "In a nutshell, the city is the best way of creating a vast open-ended social network that minimizes the cost of moving things around in an environment." He added, "When people brush up against each other, that's when the magic of the city happens—the social reactor begins to work" (Ehrenberg: 6). Cities are emergent phenomena that transform the relationships of those existing within them, and so transform the people from what they would have been had they remained in another environment.

Most of the freedom that matters, psychologically, morally, and socially, is a function of voluntary relationships that expand our realm of meaningful choices. Cities enable people of a wider variety of lifestyles to live together, and so are an easy way to experience some of the benefits of foreign travel: seeing how people different from yourself live satisfying lives, and thereby enlarging your awareness of choice. Cities are usually the social environments most tolerant of individual differences. They are most receptive to unorthodox ideas and creative thinking. They transform the people who live within them, and are one more step in the long chain of gradually complexifying relationships that expand the freedom and diversity of human life itself.

Most creation takes existing elements and recombines them. An environment rich with contrasting elements that are able to be combined in an unknown number of new ways is more conducive to creative choices than one that is not.

The issue is not people's preferring income to freedom. Past a certain point, most of us would, but this misunderstands the basic issue. Freedom must include all three moments in Berger and Luckmann's model. For one thing, it must be a realm of voluntary interactions. Here the methodological individualist model is insightful.

But as my Crusoe example demonstrated, these interactions must be available. Being "free" on a desert island is not a realm of human freedom because human beings are irreducibly social. Freedom in society is a realm of voluntary *social* relations. The richer the variety of voluntary relations into which a person can enter, the richer the realm of freedom. Crusoe's freedom enlarged when he met Friday, even though it meant he was to some degree constrained compared to before he met Friday. When he was rescued, this realm of relations available to him expanded dramatically as did the rules he had to live under.

Further, a free society is one that transmits these conditions to the next generation. It seeks to preserve and perhaps even enhance the realm of voluntary relationships into which its members can enter.

But what of the claim that with no regulations urban freedom would be even greater? An easy answer would be to send all GMU economists making this argument to Beijing to teach for some decades and breathe the air. Unregulated air is free air, so they will enjoy at least this dimension of freedom compared to the oppression of breathing regulated air in the United States.

But there is a less rhetorical reply as well.

The realm of enriched relationships made possible by urban environments *also* intensifies many human interactions that are *not* desirable, particularly unintended ones. In addition, the face-to-face relationships that could lead to reducing these problems is weak or lacking. As people live in more continuous and complex relationship with their environment and with one another, what constitutes legitimate behavior changes. I can play loud music in the country and not annoy people to the degree I annoy them doing the same thing in a city. My auto exhaust contributes imperceptibly to anyone's discomfort, but in a large urban area taken together all our exhaust can be lethal for some. This and similar phenomena are why cities are far more filled with regulations about pollution, noise, and building codes, to name three, than the countryside They are far more intrusive and far more necessary, than in rural regions. California and New York are far more urban than North Dakota or indeed any of the five "freest" states, as the size of their largest cities (rounded to nearest thousand) eloquently demonstrates. And the "freest" has the smallest largest city and the smallest population.

Without arguing that all regulations are public spirited, for they obviously are not, many are. To give a prosaic example, wood stoves were fine in Missoula, Montana, until populations reached such a level that in winter smoke from stoves became a health hazard due to wintertime temperature inversions. Then Missoula's citizens were forced to confront

Table 2.1

"Freest" States	
Largest City	Total Population
ND: Fargo – 106,000	700,000
SD: Sioux Falls – 150,000	833,000
NH: Manchester – 110,000	1,321,000
TN: Memphis – 674,000	6,456,000
OK: Oklahoma City – 599,000	3,815,000
"Least Free" States	
NY: New York – 8,244,000	19,570,000
CA: Los Angeles – 3,780,000	38,040,000

(Data from Mercatus, 2013)

a problem they had never faced before. They addressed it by changing the bundle of rights regarding stoves and fireplaces. As Missoula grew from a small town into a small city, the richness of relationships available to its residents increased. Freedom for human beings grew. But with this increase came transformations generating negative phenomena requiring a rethinking of what relationships between individuals and their property were legitimate.

There are countless examples of such modifications arising from changed conditions.

Blanket statements about regulations limiting "freedom" are fundamental misunderstandings of the nature of human life, misunderstandings made far easier by an overreliance on methodological individualism. Most people feel freer in large cities than in rural environments. They are right to feel this way.

My point is not that cities are always the best place in which to live. The freedom I am describing is important, but for most people, beyond a certain level it is not all important, a point even defenders of the GMU study apparently grant, even if they only grasp its significance in terms of income. Having a rich realm of freedom varies in importance during a person's life. Freedom is an important value, but it is not the only important value, and all normal people choose to limit their freedom of choice at different times in their lives, as when they get married or have families. It makes sense from my analysis that young people are attracted to urban environments, and many older people, having created their lives and made the choices most central in becoming who they are, often prefer different places less rich in such options.

Appropriate Relationships

The issue of property rights and regulation underlies my examples of air in Beijing and Missoula. The meaning of property and property rights takes on new depths of meaning when treated from within an emergent ecological framework. Methodological individualist analysis in economics treats property as a means for contractual exchanges. This is true as far as it goes, but it does not go very far.

In an economic sense, property is not a thing. It is a "bundle" of discrete rights, and this bundle can be disaggregated (Demsetz, 1967). For example, when I rent an apartment, my landlord owns the building, but so long as I pay my rent, he sells me the conditional exclusive right to use some aspects of that building. He no longer can enter whenever he wants, as he could when he possessed the entire bundle. Bundles can also be fragmented and some parts sold permanently. In the case of conservation easements, the landowner sells some rights unconditionally to another, but continues to own the rest.

Bundles of property rights consist of what is regarded as the *appropriate range of relationships* regarding the property that I might enter into, or not. I find it telling that methodological individualist analysis of exchange simply assumes property rights exist, without inquiring into what should be part of the bundle, and what should not. Even the explicit recognition that property was a bundle came only in the late '60s. Yet normal human beings distinguish these legitimate relationships quite differently from one context to another. Nearly all of us would agree my bundle of property rights constituting "owning my pencil" properly differs from my property rights regarding "owning my pets."

If property rights are determined by what are considered legitimate relations between a person and what is owned, as relationships within a society change, new phenomena can and sometimes will emerge. They can transform what are considered legitimate relationships regarding property's use. Air and water quality, noise ordinances, height limitations, and the many other regulations of urban life arise from people's being more tightly intertwined than in the country. Urban communities then have to revisit traditional property rights and determine what relationships are appropriate under new circumstances and what relationships are not. Of course, there is no guarantee the correct decisions will be made, but that is quite another issue from whether they need to be made or not.

Conclusion

Hayek's shift from methodological individualism to a more nuanced understanding of individuals as both shaping and being shaped by social relationships, many of which were in no way matters of choice, was an important early step in a transformation of how we understand what it is to be a human being in the world and in society. This transformation does not so much have ideological content as it reframes the context in which we think about ideologies and what constitutes values such as freedom and the individual. It is time to demote methodological individualism from its primary role in much social science thinking into being one (important) "moment" among three in the emergent processes that shape all life on earth, including our own. The intellectual watershed Hayek helped open to our view not only vastly expands our ability to understand human society but also vastly increases our understanding of how society might be encouraged to become more beneficial to us all.

REFERENCES

Agence France-Presse. 2012. "Chemical Exposure Influences Rat Behavior for Generations." *The Raw Story*, May b22, http://www.rawstory.com/rs/2012/05/22/chemical-exposure-influences-rat-behavior-for-generations/.

Axelrod, Robert. 2006. *The Evolution of Cooperation*. New York: Basic Books.

Barton, Jo and Jules Pretty. 2010. "What Is the Best Dose of Nature and Green Exercise for Improving Mental Health? A Multi-study Analysis." *Environmental Science and Technology*, 44(10): 3947–3955, http://pubs.acs.org/doi/abs/10.1021/es903183r.

Berger, Peter and Thomas Luckmann. 1967. *The Social Construction of Reality: A Treatise on the Sociology of Knowledge*. New York: Anchor.

Cacioppo, J. T., J. H. Fowler, and N. A. Christakis. 2009. "Alone in the Crowd: The Structure and Spread of Loneliness in a Large Social Network." *Journal of Personality and Social Psychology*, 97: 977–991.

Caldwell, Bruce. 2004. *Hayek's Challenge: An Intellectual Biography of F. A. Hayek*. Chicago: University of Chicago Press.

Callahan, Gene. 2013. "Liberty versus Libertarianism." *Politics, Philosophy & Economics*, 12(1): 48–67, http://ppe.sagepub.com/content/12/1/48.full.pdf.

Carson, Rachel. 1962. *Silent Spring*. New York: Houghton Mifflin.

Chan, W. H., C. Gumot, T. J. Montine, J. A. Sonnen, K. A. Guthrie, and J. L. Nelson. 2012. "Male Microchimerism in the Human Female Brain." *PLoS One*, 7(9), http://www.ncbi.nlm.nih.gov/pubmed/23049819.

Christakis, Nicholas A., and James H. Fowler. 2009. *Connected: The Surprising Power of Our Social Networks and How They Shape Our Lives*. New York: Little Brown and Company.

———. 2008. "Social Networks and Happiness." *Edge*, December 4. http://edge.org/conversation/social-networks-and-happiness.

Demsetz, Harold. 1967. "Toward a Theory of Property Rights." *American Economic Review*, 57: 347–359.

Dias, Brian G. and Kerry J. Ressler. 2014. "Parental Olfactory Experience Influences Behavior and Neural Structure in Subsequent Generation." *Nature Neuroscience*, 17: 89–96, http://www.nature.com/neuro/journal/v17/n1/nn.3594/metrics-auth-2.

diZerega, Gus. 2014. "Contract, Freedom, and Flourishing: The Implications of Spain's Mondragon Cooperatives." In Guinevere Nell (ed.), *Austrian Theory and Economic Organization*, pp. 123–146. New York: Palgrave Macmillan.

———. 2013. "Outlining a New Paradigm." *Cosmos and Taxis: Studies in Emergent Order and Organization*, I(1), 3–20.

———. 2000. *Persuasion, Power and Polity: A Theory of Democratic Self-Organization*. Cresskill, NJ: Hampton Press, 2000.

———. 1997. "Market Non-neutrality: Systemic Bias in Spontaneous Orders." *Critical Review*, 2(1): 121–144, http://www.tandfonline.com/doi/abs/10.1080/08913819708443447?journalCode=rcri20#preview.

Dobbs, David. 2007. "The Green Space Cure: The Psychological Value of Biodiversity," November 13, http://www.scientificamerican.com/blog/post/the-green-space-cure-the-psychologi/.

Durkheim, Émile. 1997. *Suicide: A Study in Sociology*. New York: Free Press.

Haeffel, Gerald J. and Jennifer L. Hames, 2013. "Cognitive Vulnerability to Depression Can Be Contagious." *Clinical Psychological Science*, 2, 75–85.

Hayek, F. A. 1988. "The Fatal Conceit: The Errors of Socialism." In W. W. Bartley III (ed.), *The Collected Works of F.A. Hayek*. Chicago: University of Chicago Press.

———. 1979. *Law Legislation and Liberty, Vol. III: The Political Order of a Free People*. Chicago: University of Chicago Press.

———. 1948. *Individualism and Economic Order*, Chicago: University of Chicago Press.

Herro, Alana. 2007. "Biodiversity Can Provide Mental Health Benefits," Worldwatch Institute, May 30, http://www.worldwatch.org/node/5096.

Hurley, Dan. 2013. "Grandma's Experiences Leave a Mark on Your Genes." *Discover*, June 11.

Jacobs, Jane. 1961. *The Death and Life of Great American Cities*. New York: Random House.

Lewis, Paul. 2010. "Peter Berger and His Critics: The Significance of Emergence." *Society*, 47(3): 207–213.

Lewis, Richard. 2012. "Self-awareness in Humans Is More Complex, Diffuse Than Previously Thought. University of Iowa, August 22, http://www.eurekalert.org/pub_releases/2012-08/uoi-sih081712.php.

Macy, Joanna. 1991. *Mutual Causality in Buddhism and General Systems Theory*. Albany: State University of New York Press.

Mann, C. 1991. "Lynn Margulis: Science's Unruly Earth Mother." *Science*, 252(5004): 378–381.

Margulis, Lynn, 1970, *Origin of Eukaryotic Cells*. New Haven: Yale University Press.

Martone, Robert. 2012. "Scientists Discover Children's Cells Living in Mothers' Brains," *Scientific American*, December 4, http://www.scientificamerican.com/article/scientists-discover-childrens-cells-living-in-mothers-brain/.

McFall-Ngai, Margaret et al. 2013. "Animals in a Bacterial World: A New Imperative for the Life Sciences." *Proceedings of the National Academy of Science*, February 26.

Mercatus Center. 2013. *Freedom in the 50 States*, http://freedominthe50states.org/.

Milius, Susan. 2014. "Microscopic Menagerie." *Science News*, January 11.

Mises, Ludwig. 2011. *Socialism: An Economic and Sociological Analysis*. Auburn, AL: Ludwig von Mises Institute.

———. 2007. *Human Action*. Indianapolis: Liberty Fund.

New Scientist. 2013. "How Mum's Stress Affects Her Fetus," November 23.

Noë, Alva. 2009. *Out of Our Heads: Why You Are Not Your Brain, and Other Lessons from the Biology of Consciousness*. New York: Hill and Wang.

Ouimet, Maeghan. 2012. "Is California Losing Start-ups to Other States?" *Inc.*, September 26, http://www.inc.com/maeghan-ouimet/silicon-alley-soon-to-best-silicon-valley.html.

Pentland, Alex, 2014. "The Death of Individuality." *New Scientist*, April 5, 30–31.

Polanyi, Michael. 1958. *Personal Knowledge*. Chicago: University of Chicago Press.
Pretty, Jules. 2010. "A Walk a Day Keeps the Doctor Away," University of Essex, Colchester Campus, May 2, http://www.essex.ac.uk/news/event.aspx?e_id=1588.
Rothbard, Murray N. 1970. *Power and Market: Government and the Economy.* Menlo Park, CA: Institute for Humane Studies.
Sanders, Laura. 2013. "Pregnant Mom's Stress Alters Baby," *Science News*, December 14, 13.
———. 2013. "Fear Can Be Inherited: Parents' and Even Grandparents' Experiences Echo in Offspring." *Science News,* December 1, https://www.sciencenews.org/article/fear-can-be-inherited?mode=magazine&context=187836.
Sanford, Peter. 2010. "How to Change Your Life in Five Minutes a Day: Go Outside." *The Independent*, May 9. http://www.independent.co.uk/opinion/commentators/peter-stanford-how-to-change-your-life-in-five-minutes-a-day-go-outside-1969209.html.
ScienceDaily. 2010. "Can Bacteria Make You Smarter?" American Society for Microbiology, May 25, www.sciencedaily.com/releases/2010/05/100524143416.htm.
Scott, James C. 1998. *Seeing Like a State*, New Haven: Yale University Press.
Shugart, Jessica. 2014. "Mother Lode." *Science News*, January 11.
Saey, Tina Hesman. 2013. "Your Body Is Mostly Microbes." *Science News*, December 18, 19.
Slezak, Michael. 2014. "No Viruses? No Skin or Bones Either." *New Scientist,* March 1.
Sober, E. and D. S. Wilson. 1988. *Unto Others: The Evolution and Psychology of Unselfish Behavior*. Cambridge, MA: Harvard University Press.
Stanford Encyclopedia of Philosophy. 2010. *Methodological Individualism*, November 16, http://plato.stanford.edu/entries/methodological-individualism/.
Wilson, E. O. 2012. *The Social Conquest of the Earth*. New York: W. W. Norton.
Yevtushenko, Yevgeny. 1979. *Selected Poems* New York: Penguin.
Zimmer, Carl. 2013. "DNA Doubletake." *New York Times*, September 17. http://www.nytimes.com/2013/09/17/science/dna-double-take.html?pagewanted=all&_r=0.
Zwicki, Todd. 2000. "Was Hayek Right about Group Selection After All?" Review Essay of *Unto Others: The Evolution and Psychology of Unselfish Behavior*, by Elliott Sober and David Sloan Wilson. *Review of Austrian Economics*, 13: 81–95.

PART 2

SPONTANEOUS ORDER AND SOCIETY

CHAPTER 3

SPONTANEOUS ORDER AND THE SOCIAL INDIVIDUAL: HAYEK, DEMOCRACY, AND PUBLIC CHOICE*

GUINEVERE LIBERTY NELL

INTRODUCTION

Assumptions about self-interest underlie much of economic analysis; what would happen if human nature or culture changed, perhaps became more enlightened as discussed by Nell (this volume), and voters began to vote more for the common good than their own personal interests, and representatives began to care more about doing what is right than about personal payoffs? This would result in the end of "public choice" economics and the Austrian analysis that relies on it.

Because the choices people make are affected by the formal and informal institutions in question, the assumptions we make about public and private sector efficiency may be based on a historically contingent "human nature." This was Karl Marx's argument. Marx (1959 [1844]) argued that human nature was shaped by the historical conditions that prevail, especially the ownership of the means of production. Marx said, "a new mode of production and a new object of production" create "a new

* I want to thank Andy Denis for some very helpful comments on an earlier draft. Remaining errors and omissions are of course my own.

manifestation of the forces of human nature and a new enrichment of human nature" and since man was a social being, and property alienated man, common ownership would erase the antagonism between individuals, leading to a new man and a new society.

Could Marx have been right about this? Because culture cannot change overnight, it may be that these choices are predictable in broad outlines for the effect of immediate changes to institutions (i.e., when a policy change is pushed through forcefully, rather than as a result of a prior cultural change and democratic vote). There is much evidence that Austrians were correct regarding the effect of Marxist policies in the Soviet Union (Nell, 2010). However, over the longer term the cultural and social changes may mean that the old assumptions no longer apply to the same degree—and eventually may cease to offer any predictive power. If cultural and social change precede policy change, the results may be far superior, as human reaction and response may be more in line with what is required for the policy to be effective and efficient. Sanford Ikeda describes the Austrian market process theory developed by Israel Kirzner as follows:

> The central role of the entrepreneur in the market process illuminates the nature of this process itself. For if the role of entrepreneurship is to discover and eliminate pockets of ignorance in the catallaxy, then it follows that where such pockets have been eliminated there will be no scope for entrepreneurship. Assuming no further changes in the underlying data, the tendency of entrepreneurship to eliminate all pockets of ignorance tends also to bring about its own demise. (Ikeda, 1990: 78)

Hence, although "Kirzner's aim was to show that through the concept of 'alertness' one can 'incorporate entrepreneurship into the analysis without surrendering the heart of microeconomic theory,'"(Vaughn, 1994: 148), in his model, as Ikeda highlights, entrepreneurship is not much more possible than it is in mainstream neoclassical models of perfect competition. In fact, the market is a cyclical process—a dynamic and evolutionary process, in which all elements are endogenously molded. Economic agents, institutions, culture and the firms and organizations in the economy are all molded by the system, while the system itself also emerges from them. Democratic process theory posits the same about the spontaneous democratic order that Austrians argue about the market order. The difference is that the democratic order is driven by public agreement instead of private profit. The details about this process and its features must unfold during its study, but knowledge uncovered through public conversation is likely to play a central role, while voting and other tools studied by public choice and mainstream political science may play little or even no role at all.

Austrians tend to agree with the public choice school about human nature. This is rooted in their particular application of methodological individualism, which finds its origin in Ludwig von Mises' *Human Action*. F. A. Hayek explored evolution of culture and the discovery of knowledge, leading him to a model of an evolving mind and person, as well as culture and society. Hayek's own ideas evolved over time, and sometimes (arguably) strayed from the conclusions of his mentor, Mises (see Salerno, 1993; Horwitz, 1998; cf. also Denis, this volume).

The pure methodological individualism of the Mises School fails to allow for possible directions that the Hayekian evolution could take. The Austrian school relies upon self-interested individualism and therefore public choice school assumptions, and the conclusions that come from that school. The public choice school relies upon this strict methodological individualism and therefore suggests only one narrow possible outcome of the evolution of a Hayekian spontaneous order–based society.

The market order is evolutionary (see also DiZerega and Camplin, this volume), but is usually defended by Austrians purely along economic dimensions, with culture offering support for economic growth.[1] The social evolution that Hayek talks about allows for a breaking out from the pure self-interested action of the individual of the Misesian and public choice school assumptions; society and culture affect the way that we act by providing other, more social, reasons for action. The conclusions of the Austrian school should be modified to take account of Hayek's understanding of evolving social orders, and with this understanding to recognize potentially efficient ways of utilizing public property institutions in an evolutionary democratic spontaneous order that is analyzable with a democratic process theory. Markets based purely on private property are not necessary for economic efficiency; and bureaucracy, corruption, rent-seeking, and power-seeking are not the only possible outcomes from public ownership.

Individualism, Utilitariansim, and Solidarism

In an article about utilitarianism and individualism, libertarian scholar Matthew Zwolinski (2008: 148–149) explains two conclusions that have come from the consideration of the individual *as such*, or the "separateness" of the individual: one school says that "it must support assigning lexical priority to the claims of the worst-off individual," and the other holds a "general objection to balancing benefits and harms in one life with benefits and harms in another." Notably, Austrians would deny the first, and they also argue the second (the impossibility of interpersonal utility comparisons).

Zwolinski argues that the importance of individualism is in the "basic moral status of individuals under the theory" (2008: 149), but the "decision procedure" of the utilitarian focuses on the aggregate of many completely separate individuals, undermining its ability to respect these separate individuals as such. This decision procedure, he says, ignores the moral value of the person, counting them merely as a number. According to Zwolinski, it is whether there is respect for the individual and refusal "to subordinate them for the sake of the greater good" that determines the nature of the liberal society (2008: 149). Although Marx and his followers may have similarly promised to value the individual in communism (the future society that was their goal), their ethics and their plan for bringing about this future, departed from this ideal. Their attempts at "making socialists," for example, put society before the individual, because they believed that this would help bring individual and social interests in line with each other, and help the individual become his true, enlightened potential (see Nell, 2014a).[2]

The utilitarian decision procedure also omits the person as *more* than a completely separate individual, as a part of a larger web of persons. The Lucas Critique was the argument that policy changes influence actions and anticipations, and hence the macroeconomic outcome of models. Hence, as Cameron K. Murray of the "Fresh Economic Thinking" blog (2014) put it, "unless you model the macro economy as a result of 'deep parameters' of the human psyche, you will never be sure whether your model will apply in a different regulatory or institutional environment." This critique of the macroeconomic models of the time led to the "microfoundations" revolution. However, Murray (2014) points out,

> Overcoming the Lucas Critique is apparently achieved by offering a macroeconomic model that stems from a utility function of a representative agent.
>
> But why should we believe that the "deep parameters" of microfoundations, the utility functions themselves, are somehow independent of the institutional environment?
>
> You can't escape Lucas' critique by plucking a utility function out of the air and giving it to a representative agent unless you believe that utility functions are independent of the social environment. Which raises the question, how can it be possible for an individual's preferences, their utility function, to arise in a social vacuum?

The interaction between persons results in their existence as not completely separate but actually socially dependent, interacting persons. Their personalities and choices are constituted by their social setting, which is in turn created by the many interactions of the past. Each individual exists in a context in relation to every other person, which means that we should not make a utilitarian calculation based solely on the supposed (static) utility or the assumed preferences of completely separate individuals. If we do, we will lose this web of social interchange. We will *devalue* it as economists.

If this perspective is then shared with the people, through the public acknowledgment of this method of economic inquiry or its use in public policy, the devaluation of social exchange relationships may ultimately corrode the culture. Economists are part of public debate, with think tanks in Washington D.C. and many economists as public figures, and as council to the U.S. president and congress; treating individuals in this static manner affects public conversation, policy, and culture. The more weight we give to analysis based solely upon the separate utility functions and preferences of isolated individuals the more we risk devaluing, dismissing, or neglecting the culture and dynamic society that we create through interaction. In contrast, if we recognize its importance, we may utilize it to our advantage, nurture and cultivate it, avoiding the negative effects of groupthink and taking advantage of the positive effects of enlightened collaboration and association.

The way that we affect culture with institutional choice, and the way that economists and utilitarians of any discipline omit this effect, is illustrated by a study on the effect of being a torturer. Nolen Gertz (2009) shows the gap in utilitarian accounts of the use of torture: the utilitarian view on torture only considers utils gained by society for good (the information, assuming it is for the common good) and utils lost by the tortured person. It ignores the effect on the torturer and on society. This is not just because utilitarian analysis does not choose to take the broader effects of torture on society into account. This is a problem that Austrians using spontaneous order analysis should well understand: it is a problem of knowledge and the emergent forces of culture.

Even if a utilitarian analysis considers in general terms the externality of torture on society (in terms of general distaste), it cannot take into account, for we cannot even know, the full effect (1) on the torturer, or the myriad ways in which the effect on the torturer is then spread across society whenever that person who has become a torturer (2) interacts with others, (3) when torture use becomes known by others through the media, and the public become accomplices to it by knowing of it and not stopping it, and (4) the compounding effects this has throughout society.

By dividing people into separate individuals and only calculating the effects on each separately, we make the same mistake that Austrians accuse mainstream neoclassical economists of making when they consider only the "seen" effects of policy, and not the "unseen" effects upon dynamic growth and innovation: there is only consideration of the "first-round" effects upon the individuals immediately involved, and not of all those whose choices are affected by the changed "ecosystem" or the social or economic environment, respectively.

Similarly, we consider utility in cost/benefit analysis of policies and of systems, for example, looking at the productive *gains* of division of labor, and the *cost* of having to work. But what effect does hiring and firing have upon our lives? What impact is there on a society when people are made to act as boss and worker? Arguably, this creates a certain isolation and division between people—not necessarily into classes, but simply between individuals—that would not exist, or would be very different in kind, in agrarian societies, tribal societies, communes, cooperatives, and other kinds of systems. The particular isolation and division—or "alienation," as Marx (1959 [1844]) put it—required for the market to function must affect the community and help produce the culture of capitalist nations. Car culture is both an expression of and a factor in the maintenance of this isolation, and of course commercialism further affects our personalities and preferences (see Nell, 2013), and these in turn may influence how we grow and develop as individuals and as societies.

Markets produce the "work ethic" and the "productivist" culture and mentality (for good and/or ill), which is so prominent in the United States especially. A change to culture, just like a change to institutions, has the potential to reduce the value of the wealth produced by skewing production and/or consumption toward things that are valued less, including things that are valued only for their use as signals or other tools of the society.[3] Culture can have this effect if it influences individuals and groups to reduce leisure time (if "productivist" and/or "materialistic"), or by underproducing goods/services that are not valued by the economy because they have no price or have too low a price (e.g., nonmaterial things of value). The other side of this is that things that produce profit are bolstered by the system, spreading advertising and production of these goods into every corner of the Earth as commerce spreads.

Culture will tend to alter the choices made by individuals and groups and affect the manner in which they interact with each other. As Nell (2013) points out, the heavily weighted demonstration in markets of the most "productive" assures that the preferences of those favoring nonmarket consumption are crowded out by the preferences favoring markets. This affects the culture, including traditions and habits, and it also affects the environment in which people act as well as the atmosphere within which decisions are made by individuals and groups.

In David Prychitko's *Why Economists Disagree*, William Waters presents "Social Economics: A Solidarist Perspective," in which he describes a mainstream neoclassical line of economic reasoning, a "hard core" of mainline theory that derived from classical liberals, and a completely distinct solidarist line:

> The hard core of solidarism is an alternative to the classics. It is, in fact, older than classicism. To repeat [solidarist Goetz] Briefs' phrase, it is the ethos "of the previous state of society from which liberals emancipated themselves." (Waters, 1998: 183)

Waters argues that a realistic model of the economy must focus on the mechanism of change resulting from the creative activity of the people making up that economy. Austrians would agree with this dynamic model and the modeling of the creative person. However, Austrians would not agree with the solidarist model in other respects, for example, its origin for human nature in the historical period.[4] The foundational debate between early Austrian thinkers and the German historical school was over this issue.

Waters (1998: 180–181) describes a "hard core" of mainline economics. It is, in the main, shared by "bourgeois" economic theory, including mainstream neoclassical, neo-Keynesian (although Waters argues that Keynes himself might be exempt), and Austrian theory. The "hard core" named by Waters includes four parts: (1) "the law of nature," which is the self-regulation of the economy; (2) "the individual," as the basic unit of the economy that is subject to the law of nature as she pursues her own self-interest; (3) "certainty"; and (4) "contracts," or property law.

The individual, who is subject to the law of nature via her self-interest, Waters explains, is considered not to be disruptive to the economy, but is kept in check through competition and informed by "the impersonal forces of the market" (1998: 180). Austrians clearly agree with these first two parts of the core. The last part is the assumption of property law and voluntary transactions using negotiated contracts, with which Austrians agree when studying markets. The third aspect of the "hard core"—which may be the one least adhered to by Austrians—is that of the certainty of economists and their models (although surely every economist must hold to it to some degree, or why would they bother with their craft?). Waters describes the hubris of mainstream economists:

> By the great powers of reason, economic scientists are able to understand the workings of the economy. They have correct knowledge of its relevant features. Uncertainty is ruled out, allowing economic theorists to develop determinate models and for the discipline to be acclaimed a science. (1998: 181)

Austrians working in the intellectual tradition of Lachmann (e.g., 1978) and Shackle (e.g., 1972) cannot be accused of assuming away uncertainty and claiming determinate conclusions. Many mainstream economists of the past century can. Waters (1998: 189) excludes John Maynard Keynes from his criticism; models that claim determinate outcomes are made by omitting certain variables that are unknowable, and hence make prediction impossible, such as, Waters argues, Keynes' exogenous investment variable for investment. Yet, this is still a "known unknown,"[5] and hence a variable that can have stochastic representation. Not all random (luck) factors can be known by social scientists when they analyze and produce models.

Austrians generally concede uncertainty more often, and claim to predict with determinateness less frequently, than other free market economists; however, they still (and perhaps must, as economists) assume that they are correct about the *major* features of the economy—more so in certain models than in their theory at large, but to some extent in both.[6] As "bourgeois" economists, they are confident in the regularity of the response by *self-interested individuals* in particular. This provides Austrian models with some certainty. Also, without these "core" factors, they would not come to such strong laissez-faire conclusions.

Austrians models frequently leave out of consideration features that introduce uncertainty, including, for example, the potential for spontaneous (not caused by regulation) speculative frenzy, fads, nationalistic sentiment, and other emotional (or irrational) reactions. Instead, Austrian models tend to rely on an assumption of rational choice, which is affected only by legal institutions and informal institutions that either support rational choice or hinder it and thereby reduce welfare. In theory they concede the importance of informal institutions, but they tend only to model certain possibilities. Austrians see economics as a science because they see humans as predictable: they will make the choice most in their own self-interest, and hence, for example, predictably choose the lower price, greater quantity, and so forth, unless coerced by the state (on Austrians and private coercion, see Burczak, 2013).[7] It is this that has made economics a science and allowed conclusions to be drawn, but it leaves a large portion of human nature unexamined.

On the other hand, Waters explains, *solidarists* do not see the economy as self-regulating based on self-interest. Institutions in historical context produce culture and affect how people act, react, and choose, which they often do as social unit of two or more. "Societal decision-making stems from *institutions* endowed with the values of the culture in which they are formed," according to solidarists, Waters writes (1998: 183, emphasis in original). This is, Waters asserts, "in contrast to the premises of natural lawfulness and self-regulation of conventional economics" (1998: 183). The "law of nature" is replaced with "value-laden institutions and social groups," which affect our decision-making. How society develops and how it is studied and interpreted depends upon the historical choices made by the society. The *person* (rather than the "individual") of solidarism makes decisions that are "at times rational in the calculating mold of conventional economics but are apparently more often non-rational" (Waters, 1998: 183). The self-interested individual gives way to one capable of interest in the common good; cooperation replaces competition in many cases; uncertainty is recognized; and economics is seen as a moral science, not a hard science. Finally, the person is seen to have more basic rights than merely private property rights and right to contract.

Many Austrians will likely think of Marx and earlier socialists when reading Waters' description of solidarists, above. However, there are many similarities in approach between solidarists and Austrians, and it may be worth considering the root of their divergence. Austrians already discuss where the individual's incentives come from, but this is only half the story. Where do individual preferences come from? How do people make choices? Is it really correct at all to treat the individual in isolation in models, or does this simplification undermine the validity of the model in many cases?

THE SOCIAL INDIVIDUAL

Austrians aim to model creative individuals, not automata. James Buchanan (1982), cofounder of the "public choice" school, which Austrians tend to consider a cousin school (Boettke, 2002), argues that individuals do not act on "*independently existing functions.*" Buchanan, like Mises, (1935) and Hayek (1935; 1945) before him, stressed this point within an argument about the planned economy, using it to illustrate the impossible task facing a would-be economic planner:

> I want to argue that the "order" of the market emerges *only* from the *process* of voluntary exchange among the participating individuals. The

> "order" is, itself, defined as the outcome of the *process* that generates it. The "it," the allocation-distribution result, does not, and cannot, exist independently of the trading process.
>
> Individuals do not act so as to maximize utilities described in *independently-existing functions*. They confront genuine choices. . . . The potential participants *do not know until they enter the process* what their own choices will be. From this it follows that it is *logically impossible* for an omniscient designer to know, unless, of course, we are to preclude individual freedom of will. (Buchanan 1982, italics in original)

However, Austrian theory lacks endogenous effects and relies upon public choice assumptions. It omits concern for the public good, or welfare of others, community spirit, and the effect others have on an individual. Buchanan (1982) argues that individuals do not know what their choice will be "until they enter the process" of exchange, but Austrians have not applied this to models of collective choice. If Austrians truly took seriously the idea that individuals do not know what their choice will be until they enter the process of exchange, as they understand that choice is action—and all exchange interactions, not only the economic, are analyzable within their spontaneous order system—they would also have to recognize that *any* process of exchange involves actors who do not make up their mind until the process occurs. Given this fact, they must see that the interaction is unknowable. As Lachmann terms it, there is "radical uncertainty." If the individuals do not know what they will do until the process takes place, it seems likely that the context of time and place and the interactions that occur will tend to affect the individual. Instead of self-interest driving all behavior, and selection acting upon it, compassion and kindness lend themselves to cooperation, which might also have evolutionary advantages (e.g., in Hayek's group selection). Societies may evolve that reflect this, instead of a market-centered culture and the dominance of market selection.

If individuals do not know what they will choose until they enter the exchange process, the choice is a social one. The individual is not deciding in isolation, but as part of a social exchange, or a social interaction. People decide things socially all the time—as couples (from what to have for dinner to whether to buy a house), in small groups (e.g., families, friends, clubs), and democratically or otherwise in large groups. Furthermore, the individual is a social construction. This is obvious to sociologists and psychologists, but economists tend to overlook the importance of this fact. Group decisions are what makes a "democratic process theory" so important and what makes the democratic process possible at all.

Lachmann argues that economics should be based not in individual human action (as Mises, 1949, argues) alone, but must account for the "plan" that guides this action. He argues (Lachmann, 1970) that action takes place with regard to "an unknown and unknowable future" (11) and always involves plans. "All human action, if it is to be successful, requires a plan to guide it. To understand an action means to understand the plan which is being carried out here and now"(12). As Lachmann points out, individuals each view the situation subjectively and may have different preferences, and they also view things differently over time, and may change their minds, so "Human action cannot be regarded as mere reaction to stimulus" (11).

Many actions result from plans made by groups, not individuals. When a town suffers after a large factory shuts down, or a tornado hits, or crime rises, or house prices fall, the townspeople often come together and have a meeting to decide what should be done. Once they have decided on a course of action, they might assign jobs to people, or individuals may volunteer for jobs, but either way it is only after the *group* has made a decision that these individual plans of action are drawn up. The same is true when a group of friends decides to create a business, form a music group, or begin any number of other projects—sometimes it is one individual who forms the initial idea, but quite often it is a group of individuals who decide together during the course of discussion, as Hayek recognized (see Denis, this volume).

It is a severe underestimation of the importance of social groups and culture to view them, as some economists do, as merely a matter of signaling (e.g., Murray, 2013, who says "culture is the way we understand the meaning of signals"). Other social scientists understand the importance of society to the individual's preferences, behavior, and choice:

> Sociologists . . . widely adopt models that allow for learnt behaviours of individuals through interaction with others . . . from epidemics, to racial segregation, to power in exchange networks, to evolving strategies in the prisoner's dilemma.
>
> . . . The methodological individualism so fondly embraced by the econ crowd embraces the concept of utility, but stops short of answering the far more important question—where does our utility function come from if not our environment and our interactions with others? (Murray, 2013)

Some may not see this as critically important, but when economists take preferences as given, they are missing the cycle of the system—the endogeneity and feedback, the forces at play within the system. To take preferences as given and fixed is as mistaken as taking supply costs as given and fixed—when they are of course affected by technology, which is affected by growth, which is in turn affected by institutions and policies—or any other single aspect of the dynamic, cyclical system. The individual is not a separate being from his or her surroundings, but rather has a deeply connected symbiotic relationship with it (see diZerega, this volume).[8] Austrians are suspicious of macroeconomic models that look at the effect of macro systems on each other without regard for microeconomic forces upon them.[9] But what about the reverse: models that look only at individual actions without regard for how the macroeconomic (consider culture on the one hand and inflation, investment, etc. on the other) affects them? Interactions between people, network effects, and customs and habits that come from social interaction are critical to understanding individual action. The individual should not be seen as the *origin* of his or her own preferences, since these preferences are rooted in this social network before they are taken up by the individual. Although Austrians tend to recognize that preferences are subjective and changing, they often forget that we are not born with any preferences *except* for basic necessities. In a collection of essays on free market reform in the postcommunist world, George Roche writes,

> Each of us is one of a kind, not only in mind and body, but in our talents, wants and goals. We each have a scale of values for what we want, how much we want it, and what we will do to get it. Moreover our wants and goals change constantly: We want food when we are hungry, not right after a meal. We each know what is the best thing to do according to our particular needs at a given moment, and we act on our self-knowledge; nobody else knows, and nobody else can decide for us. No two of us ever have quite the same scale of values directing what we do. (Roche, 1994: 129)

Austrians stress the subjective nature of preferences, and even note that they change over time, but not that they form and change in a social context, and although they may use food and hunger in their examples, they usually omit the clear exception to the rule of unique and subjective preferences: we *all* not only want but also *need* food when we are hungry. This has important implications, which Menger (2007: 122–123) understood.

According to Austrian theory (Mises, 1949: 52), action is taken by the individual "for the removal of *felt* uneasiness"; this "uneasiness" must be the product of the individual's existing situation in the given society. Marxists, market socialists, and other heterodox economic schools have stressed this point and suggested that culture (e.g., consumerism) and possibly even human nature might be transformed under different (e.g., less profit- and self-interest-driven) economic institutions.

Austrians discuss the importance and the evolutionary nature of civil society. For example, Austrians predicted that a top-down imposition of new institutions, no matter how well-designed, may backfire when they are not culturally accepted (Coyne, 2008), whereas, even unwritten legal frameworks may function well if they are accepted by the people because they conform to tradition (Hayek, 1979: 107–108). Hence, Peter Boettke (1990: 27) responds to a criticism of the use of "given" preferences in Austrian economics by asserting that the "sophisticated individualism" used by Austrian economists "does not deny that social customs affect individual behavior." Yet, the extent of this cultural impact is always limited in Austrian models, and the individual is still treated as the origin of his or her behavior and action. As Boettke puts it, "Individuals and their choice-making activity serve as the beginning of the Austrian analysis" (1990: 27). This is because, according to Austrians, "social customs are mediated through the actions of individuals" (1990: 27), and can be analyzed only through individual action. This leads to an analysis that treats the individual in isolation, as Gus diZerega reminds us:

> Libertarian theorists, especially modern ones, ignore millennia of philosophy and well over 100 years of scientific research demonstrating beyond reasonable doubt that we are intricately interwoven with one another and with our environment. Almost every libertarian emphasizes every individual's ultimate isolation and "autonomy." That is why their social ideal is the contract, an enforceable agreement often made between complete strangers who remain strangers.
>
> Our autonomy is quite real, but it is real in the same sense that a coin really has heads. It is half of the picture. *Autonomy is one side of a coin whose other side is relationship.* (my emphasis)[10]

These two sides should be represented in Austrian theory by market process theory and democratic process theory; instead, Austrians focus on only on the market process. Austrians explicitly exclude social orders (race, class, etc.) from their models as part of their rejection of aggregation and collectivism, and their explicit focus on the individual as the source of all economic choice. They also reject the possibility that democracy and public ownership might avoid self-interested rent-seeking and offer social choice and social welfare, arguing that choice and action can only be individual, and social welfare and efficiency are maximized through free exchange of private property. Only by assuming innate preferences and an isolated individual can their conclusions be supported. So the question becomes how the social order should be incorporated into the model, and how it would change the expected outcomes of policy choices, including public provision, power-seeking and rent-seeking, vote (democracy) versus exit (market choice), and public choice school predictions.

The Rationality of Social Choice

The assumption of rational *individual* choice may be significantly altered by the recognition that many decisions are based upon unconscious action conforming to habit (Dahlsten, 2010), which is socially influenced. Much of Austrian theory can remain intact, even if rational individual behavior does not. For an example of the way an Austrian model changes when the rational choice assumption is relaxed, consider Lachmann's emphasis on radical subjectivism and uncertainty.

Lachmann's analysis led to a theoretical hole known as the "Lachmann problem" (Lewin, 2013: 14): "Action is by definition goal oriented. . . . But if outcomes are radically uncertain why are people not debilitated? How is action possible in a radically uncertain world?" The social context of the individual provides an answer: people are products of their society (they make decisions within a social context, within the *act* of exchange) and are creatures of habit; this makes them more predictable and explains how they are able to take actions in conditions of such radical uncertainty. Some of this is habit, but much of it is shaped by social and individual decisions producing an environment or culture that encourages certain kinds of choices and discourages others, whether for moral or practical reasons, or something else.

This is not merely habit, but it need not be religious or oppressive in nature. Austrians understand this. Boettke and Virgil Storr describe criticism of those who rely strictly, perhaps mathematically, upon tradition or habit as others do upon individual rationality:

> When economists do take social influences seriously, [Mark] Granovetter argues, they end up at the other extreme, as do many sociologists: with an *oversocialized* conception of individuals. They assume "that people follow customs, habits or norms automatically and unconditionally." Like Weber and the Austrians, Granovetter overcomes the pitfalls of positing either an over- or under-socialized view of the individual by maintaining that his or her behavior is *affected* by, *influenced* by, even *directed* by social structures and relations but not *determined* by them. (Boettke and Storr, 2002: 166)

This could be called the "social-individual problem," reflecting the social science version of the nature/nurture problem of psychiatrists/philosophers and biologists. It can be solved by recognizing the complexity of society, which includes the complexity of the re/action of individuals *and* the complexity of their interaction in the cycle of the spontaneous order that is society. It is easy to assume either given preferences or determination (or probability thereof) of action due to social factors such as fads, "irrational exuberance" or speculative frenzy, or other network effects—in other words, it is easy to assume that either the individual chooses in isolation or is driven to choose based on what others have chosen. But, if the latter, how did the first individual choose? If the only choice is that an individual chose based on given preferences or an individual chose based on another individual's choice, which in turn was based on *their* given preferences, then there is still an assumption of given, isolated, preferences at the root. If preferences and actions are actually social, then these options are not enough, and indeed are not correct as described. The missing characteristic is a key part of human nature, which is that it is social *in the acts of* choosing and of forming preferences. We are not like a room full of stock brokers, each making up our minds and only influencing each other through our bids and exchanges. In real-world decision-making outside of market interactions, and even in many of them, we are influenced by many other factors, social and emotional, communal and irrational.

Public programs and uses of public monies can emerge in the same way that common law, currency, language, and other social tools emerge. Austrians and public choice theorists argue that individuals always act in their own self-interest, however defined, and not in the interest of the community or the common good; therefore, when faced with public projects or principal-agent situations, the individual will choose to shirk her duties and put herself and her own interests first. On the other hand, there is the possibility of a model in which the actors do not necessarily act in their "rational" self-interest on an *individual* level, but instead cooperate and choose rules consciously within a *group*, from as small as a married couple to as large as the world culture; making choices and acting efficiently and even "rationally" without putting individual interests first.

For this model to be realistic, the culture and institutions must encourage such behavior, as indicated above. In such a society, the people may cooperate to improve the programs and rules (legislation) and the system itself (the laws and constitution), in addition to cooperating in efficiently and effectively governing and working within existing rules and laws. Especially if decentralized, the people may have a palpable appreciation for their government, and awareness that they *are* being represented and that the rules *reflect their own needs and desires*. If they do feel this way, and if the culture supports cooperation with the system, they may not choose to "shirk," as rational choice theory suggests that they will, but instead may contribute by choice, just as so many (even under a system they see as extremely flawed and unrepresentative of their wishes) choose to make the effort to vote. Public choice theory and Austrian economists struggle to explain why any individual bothers to vote, but it becomes immediately clear with the awareness of the social individual and social choice.[11]

Paying taxes is obviously a greater burden than the effort of voting, and it may always require legal sanction, but voters tend to *vote for this legal sanction*, knowing that they prefer to be made to pay taxes than to go without the benefits—to themselves and their fellow citizens—that the taxes will pay for. The greater the perceived benefits, and the greater their sense of participation in this process, the more likely that these citizens will vote for them and the taxes to support them. This is because culture, social pressures and expectations, the joy felt in taking part in social activities, and the desire to influence (even a little) the social structure and the direction of social resources, affect the individual's choice. People also understand that even if their *isolated* action is unlikely to affect the outcome, the total effect caused by themselves, their local social groups, and the movement that they will be part of—in either case, whether as a voter or a nonvoter, if they "shirked" their duty—will have a great impact. Therefore, they make a *social choice*, not an individual choice, when they choose to vote or not, and when they choose how to vote. Recognition of this also helps lay a foundation for a democratic process theory.

Austrians should question how much they rely upon *individual* rationality and self-interest as the sole conclusive factor, because it may lead to unnecessary (but possibly self-fulfilling) conclusions. An assumption of self-interest may drive a culture of self-interest (more on this below). Given the assumptions of the "hard core" based on self-interested individuals responding to incentives in a system of private property, which allows for economic prediction, one can recognize (or interpret) the history of the development of capitalism, from a system of self-interested individuals to a society of self-interested exchange—not only in the form of private competition but also in the form of rent-seeking. Waters (1998: 182) quotes Briefs, who argues that development of "the dominant liberal societies in the Western world [advance] from self-interested individualism to a society of competing vested-interested groups to one dominated and ruled by the strongest of the groups." Briefs argues that this is part of a logical, and therefore inevitable, historical progression. From today's vested-interest pluralism, historical logic will propel us to "totalism" because "a society of competing self-interest groups is unstable."

This analysis sounds much like Marxist theories of historical development, which describe and predict more and more concentration and crises, but it also comports well with much Austrian analysis (and public choice), at least the latter portion.[12] If institutions emerge from society, as Austrians argue that they do, what drives individuals to create the institutions that they do? Is rent-seeking inevitable? There might be another possible form of public sector economic activity. Could there be, for example, democratically decentralized public exchange, of a non-rent-seeking, non-centrally planned, sort?

Culture and the details of law and legislation certainly affect the kinds of actions people take, and not all of them are either command, rent-seeking, or profit-seeking—some of them are charitable, some irrational, some creative, some out of love or laziness. Of course, it may be possible to attempt to pigeonhole actions (such as those made out of love) into rent-seeking, arguing it is a self-interested action—an action done for a loved one, nepotism, seeking rents "for" ourselves because we care about those close to us—but what of actions made *out of love* rather than *for the profit of* a loved one? Seeking and receiving public funds is generally categorized by Austrians as rent-seeking, but there are many examples of work done out of love, which may be supported by a community, that cannot be called rent-seeking without stretching the definitions of "self-interest" and "rents" to cover anything and everything. Empathy and kindness are more fundamental than self-interest, cruelty, and uncaring, otherwise we would not care for our young and we would have died out long ago. Caring and responsibility have to be learned in part, in cooperation, but the underlying compassion and desire for closeness are more the human spirit than cruelty and lust for power (although a battle of wills may occur when there are disagreements). History seems to show that the evolution of humankind is moving, although it may weave its way like a drunken sailor, toward enlightenment. It may never make it all the way, but it will keep getting closer.

CULTURE, RENT-SEEKING, AND THE DEMOCRATIC PROCESS

Although economists do not always model it, there is a sense in which people assume that culture evolves and improves. Even in popular science fiction, for example, *Star Trek*, the evolution of human society continues—having left behind slavery as an abomination, humanity then proceeds to leave behind poverty, disease, and materialism. Some of these may follow from economic growth, but they are also moral decisions, and future humanity sees the mind-sets of the past as barbaric. Culture is changing all the time, and hopefully advancing, along with the economy, toward a more nurturing and a more free future. Just as Austrians frequently note that the question ought to be how we have so successfully escaped poverty not why some still remain poor, Mary Douglas (1985) points out, "the central issue is not cultural change. The amazing thing that needs to be investigated is cultural stability, whenever and wherever it is found" (1985: xxii). Richard Seel (2000) quotes Douglas and asks, "If culture is being created all the time by everybody how is it that we sense it as reasonably stable?" Indeed, why does it often seem so impossible to change culture, so that religions last thousands of years and communist "cultural revolutions" are necessary to make a dent in certain rigid social hierarchies and allow those forgotten and mistreated by society to finally be taken seriously? Seel (2000) argues that it might be possible to answer that question "using some of the insights of complexity theory, in particular by looking at emergence."

Socialists essentially argued that a social individual (affected by those around them) with evolving preferences can learn to treat others better, care about the common good, become enlightened: they called this "making socialists" (Nell, 2014a; see Nell, this volume, for a more Austrian approach to the way human nature may change). Austrians should be well aware of the endogenous nature of individual preferences. Hodgson (1998) pointed this out, but Boettke (1990) failed to accept the critique. If people are affected by others, and by the culture and society, the assumptions of the public choice school, which lead to predictions of bureaucracy, rent-seeking and other public sector inefficiencies, are not warranted. As "enlightened" (less self-interested) culture develops, laws will either lead or trail the culture, and may include new human rights, working conditions, and criminal justice provisions, as well as modifications to constitutional laws treating property and democracy.

Hayek (1979) argues that a "liberal" culture can help constrain government and rent-seeking, an "out-of-control" public sector, and a dependent populace. Culture can work in another way: it can help improve the effectiveness and efficiency of the public sector, and the choices that the people make in their democracy. Together with good institutions—laws regarding how government should function, transparency, public involvement, debating, voting, and party organization rules, for example—a culture that respects and appreciates public sector involvement in the economy might help create a useful and fruitful public sector. As Stringham and Miles (2014) point out, both Hayek (1979) and Mises (1966) argue that public opinion or ideology—culture—can help mold and constrain or expand the institutions of the society—liberal ones can constrain the state, while socialist or entitlement ideologies can help the state expand.[13] As Mises puts it, "ideology is the totality of our doctrines concerning individual conduct and social relations" (1966: 178, chapter

9, section 2) and acts as the ultimate constraint. He also defines "world view" as "all the theorems and theories guiding the conduct of certain individuals and groups . . . an interpretation of all things, and as a precept for action, an opinion concerning the best means for removing uneasiness as much as possible." (1966: 178, chapter 9, section 2). In other words, a worldview provides the expectations and interpretation of the world that shape the actions of both individuals and groups, and ideology also regards our social relationships, in addition to our individual conduct, so it too can help shape our instinctual reactions to how we are treated and how we treat others (sympathy, as Adam Smith [1759] discussed).

This worldview is created by all the individuals in the society through their relationships and associations—groups that form both voluntarily and due to circumstance, both actively (from an individual action) and as a consequence (endogenously as a result of the system). Purposeful action and consequence (with its corresponding/subsequent reaction) are two sides of a coin (interaction), just like supply and demand (exchange). The cycle within the system—the spontaneous order—has endogenous factors. Consider racism and other forms of discrimination: an individual's racism will certainly contribute to the racism of the society, and the racism around a person may contribute to an individual's opinions about race; but, also, racism about an individual can often dissipate once the person becomes known to those who discriminate, and markets can foster this, just as democracy can, or can block it. As Hayek said, "It is precisely through the disappointment of expectations that a high degree of agreement of expectations is brought about" (2002 [1968]: 15). Disagreement, debate, communication, agreement: this is the process, cyclical and evolutionary, that produces what we tend to call democracy and must investigate with some form of "democratic process theory."

Austrians offer an attempt at an evolutionary model (Hayek, 1979), but omit the effects of learning from mistakes, knowledge accumulation, and evolutionary social change in the public sector (see also, Nell, 2014a). Hayek models culture as an evolutionary spontaneous order, which evolves through a process of group selection, but he does not explore the effect of culture on public sector incentives, or other outcomes of evolving social preferences. Although Hayek (1960) discusses the effects that culture and religion may have on the size and kind of public sector in a society, he fails to note how else culture might affect public programs. A society with greater public awareness of policy, and a culture of caring for those in need, will have very different public policy outcomes than one without. Austrian economists have argued that money emerges from barter and that the market economy is a spontaneous order, whereas a planned economy is imposed upon the people. The political process may also be a spontaneous order in a democracy. Austrians argue that such a spontaneous order would likely be inefficient as it would be captured by rent-seeking by legislators interested only in their own constituency, or interest groups seeking their own interests, rather than the common good.[14] Legislative decisions may emerge through a process similar to an auction, with legislators "bidding" for certain legislation. Hence, the way for a spontaneous order to produce good results must be either for sectional interests to lead to good results (given the institutions) or for the parties not to seek sectional interests.[15]

Tullock (2005) argues that ideology is critical to good lawmaking, and that ideology can foster rent-seeking within lawmaking; ideology has a role in determining whether common law is driven by rent-seeking or by wealth-maximizing goals. Propaganda influences a people, through their culture, to believe in the goals of the state, but this is a top-down force; there are also cultural changes that are bottom-up, like riots and popular revolutions, as well as changes in religious belief and social norms. This is the same argument that Hayek made in his *Constitution of Liberty*. Hayek (1960: 109, 314) argues that a strong culture of liberal enlightenment ideology will keep a democracy contained, possibly better than any constitution could do; culture is critical for institutions to function as expected.

If Hayek had continued working along these lines, adding his later insights on cultural evolution to this line of reasoning, he might have introduced a democratic process theory and had greater respect for the potential for efficient and effective public provision, and less stringent belief in self-interest-based public choice considerations (see also Nell, 2014b). Whether individuals are self-interested or hold social considerations (the common good) higher than personal ends might determine whether or not (or to what extent) a spontaneously ordered use of public funds will be driven by rent-seeking. Instead, Austrians argue that individuals are always driven by interest, and that the more crucial consideration affecting the outcome, in addition to the particular incentives of the institutions, is whether policy is created endogenously (evolving within the society) or imposed from the outside.

Hayek (1979) argues that the common law system produced superior results to civil law because it emerged spontaneously, whereas civil law was a top-down legal system imposed upon a society; however Tullock (2005) models the development of the common law system as rent-seeking parties pleading for favors and argues that this is unlikely to produce socially beneficial results. If rent-seeking pressures within the legislative decision-making process lead to rent-dissipation with random results, the development of the common law system is unlikely to lead to an efficient outcome; whereas if the bottom-up emergence of common law is likely to produce good results, then a bottom-up, endogenously created legislative process should also produce a more efficient outcome.

If "liberal" (market) culture can support market societies by reducing the costs of enforcing rule of law, restrain the growth of welfare by reducing entitlement mentality and increasing responsibility and entrepreneurial values—if, as Boettke argues, it is a tool for the self-regulation of behavior—then culture should be able to reduce costs in the public sector too. Culture could help reduce public choice considerations, including corruption—not only by reducing the growth of government, as Hayek (1960) argues, but by reducing bad behavior in the government—and other of the negative outcomes predicted by Austrians and the public choice school. A "socialist" or "democratic" culture might reduce bureaucracy by helping ensure that *public* property is respected, public programs are efficiently governed, corruption is held in check by social norms, transparency, and effective rules against it, and that administrators act as civil servants. It might also put boundaries upon the selfish drive for profit and help transform the *market* system into a less profit-based and more cooperative society.

For example, both Austrians and market socialists often agree that profit-seeking will quash attempts at cooperative-based or other nonprofit societies, because profit-seeking companies will outcompete firms not focused on profit; however, if institutional tools and resources are available to help nonprofits, and there is a culture that is against putting nonprofits out of business, this may not be the case. In a society that limits profit, it might be possible for a cooperative society to emerge; in one that refuses to allow unethical businesses to become, or to remain, profitable, an ethical-market society might be possible. Austrians offer many reasons why limiting profit is dangerous (limiting just extraordinary profits may reduce these dangers, of course); these are merely examples of possible ways of guiding the market system with a change in the property laws. There are also ways of harnessing the powers of the public property spontaneous order.

Democratic process theory, like market process theory, must define the institutions and incentives that drive the self-perpetuating system, as well as the features and tools that maximize its efficiency and effectiveness. Just as competition is a core feature of markets, helping to convey information (through prices) and provide incentives for efficiency (though profit and loss), conversation is a core feature of democracy, helping to convey information (through public debate and discussion, and finally votes) and provide incentives for efficiency (through elections and the threat of recall, for example). As diZerega explains, democracy is not merely about voting:

> [majority rule democracy] seems to suggest the hierarchical subjection of a minority to a majority. This unease often comes from equating the final vote with democracy. In reality, however, democracy encompasses the total process of discussion, debate, and voting. (diZerega, 2011: 182)

As diZerega reminds us, "Equating democracy with the final vote is akin to equating the market with a consumer's final purchase" (2011: 182). Austrians should know better than to make this substitution; markets are a process that offers much more than the final purchase—the whole knowledge discovery procedure, including the provision of goods through the supply chain, occurs before each final purchase. Democracy need not even be based on majority rule, and in many societies, discussion, and even unanimity, have played a much larger role than they do in Western democracies today (Graeber, 2004).

Just as there can be greater or lesser competition in a market, and people hold differing views about how it should be guarded or encouraged, the public conversation (including but by no means limited to voting and elections) is a parallel feature of democracy. Just as competition requires certain attributes of markets, including freedom from government controls and mandates (such as on prices) and free entry and exit, public conversation requires attributes of the democratic system, including transparency and accountability, and just as with markets, free entry and exit. The "two-party system" of the United States is an example of a democratic system sorely lacking this attribute. It is extremely difficult for a newcomer without close ties to the highest ranking member of one of the parties to enter, with any chance of winning, any political race above town councilperson. Of course, in both the market and the democratic system, what is technically (de jure) possible, such as "entry" into the sphere—market or democracy—in question, and what is meaningfully (de facto), possible, may have little in common.

James Bohman (2006) writes of the importance of diversity for deliberative democracy, arguing that diversity has three aspects: the diversity of opinions, values, and perspectives. According to Bohman, it is the availability of perspectives, the *inputs* to the conversation, that ought to be maximized—not the policy proposals, or other outputs, which the public is to vote on. Diversity of opinions for the democratic process depends upon certain prerequisites such as: an open and flexible culture (see also Nell, chapter 6 in this volume); relatively open borders; lack of censorship; accessibility of media to the public for sharing their thoughts, ideas, and criticism; civil and constructive public discussion (not just sound bites, insults, and lies); and an informed and educated public. Finally, for the "outputs," the diversity of policy, there must be an actual ability for multiple parties or groups to offer a diversity of policy ideas, and worldviews or perspectives, and they must have both a platform and a true chance of winning enough votes for their proponents to take office and represent the people who believe in them. Analysis and investigation of the full list of requirements, part of a (post-) Austrian "democratic process theory," in conjunction with "new democratic theory" (see Gagnon, 2014), should help improve public sector potential efficiency.

Could enlightened thinking of the public also improve a spontaneously ordered public-resource-using collective action project? The socialist theory is that the "tragedy of the commons" problem need not plague production under common ownership; it can be combated so long as the workers are made to feel ownership over common property and are given true democratic control. The democracy and equality granted the people help foster the feeling of control, which in turn helps them become enlightened and put their full mental and physical efforts into making the best use of those resources. Austrians have traditionally argued that this is unrealistic because humans are self-interested by their (fixed) nature. However, as outlined above, there is good reason to believe that both preferences/choice and action/reaction are in part endogenous features of the system in question: Many choices are made socially and people are social beings. This line of reasoning may even begin to lay a bridge between Marxism and Austrian theory via the work of Elinor Ostrom, whose scholarship helps elucidate the features of efficient common ownership societies.

OSTROM AND THE AUSTRIANS

Actions are made for reasons, and other people's actions—which together constitute the social order, or culture—critically affect our decisions. A *culture* of self-interest may be essential to development of a society with significant rent-seeking. Such a society may also be encouraged by the collection of individuals into groups, as interest groups will have more power to obtain rents than individuals acting alone. These combined forces—self-interest and collective action in interest groups—together may propel a society along a rent-seeking path, which may then build its own momentum (Krueger, 1974).

This result *necessarily* must be based on an abundance of self-interested parties—people pleading for favors for themselves or their interest groups (although some of the individuals may plead on behalf of others, sometimes loved ones are in disadvantaged positions). There must be a critical mass, such as to reach a tipping point that forces those who are reluctant to act in their self-interest to do so in order to survive (Nell, 2011). If instead the people are more interested in the *common* good, because (1) the *culture* expects people to seek the common good, (2) the legal *institutions* are designed to serve the common good, and (3) *the public conversation is dedicated to discovering and bringing about* the common good, then the result will be the emergence of knowledge of this good and public programs with a fair chance of achieving it, rather than the emergence of rent-seeking.

These discoveries may come from decentralized democracy and transparency in public debate, emerging through, for example, Internet innovations and political parties such as the Pirate Party's Liquid Democracy in Germany (Meyer, 2012), from petitions and discussion groups, and experiments from co-operatives (as small as single-building housing co-ops to as large as Mondragon in Spain; see diZerega's chapter in Nell, 2014c) to SeaSteading (http://www.seasteading.org) to innovative ideas such as firms run like profit-seeking companies but giving up all their profits to a cause, the example of this being One Water (http://onedifference.org). These all relate to the "important work by Elinor Ostrom," which

> highlighted the importance and success of endogenously emergent institutional solutions to a range of coordination problems, as well as the potential for unintended, undesirable outcomes when political authorities artificially construct institutional solutions to these problems. (Boettke, Coyne, and Leeson 2008: 333)

As Austrians are well aware, "the endogenous emergence of the institution points to its desirability as seen from indigenous inhabitants' point of view" (338). This means that endogenously emerging public programs that coevolve with the culture should be more efficient and better managed than ones, for example, imposed by an external body, such as the World Bank or the European Union. Similarly, a more local government body's programs, emerging from the local culture rather than a more distant government, should perform better. Austrians argue for the efficiency of decentralization in part because of knowledge problems. As Ostrom (1990) argues, and Austrians have long argued, a distant government will not know the needs and resources of each local community.

The democratic process may turn out to be more a mode of communication and a form of organization than a specific set of institutions; with transparency and flexibility, communication networks can be added to exchange as a way of allocating resources and distributing the output of society.[16]

This line of inquiry is a natural outgrowth of the study by economists of the effects of culture and society, and full recognition of the issues involved should lead Austrians to recognize that public provision can be significantly more efficient under conditions of decentralized democratic accountability, emergent legislation within a culture that appreciates the local governance, and transparency and public conversation. Unless they can convincingly argue that such conditions are an outright impossibility, there is no excuse for the lacuna in their program where a "democratic process theory" should be, nor for the brazen assumptions often made that all public programs must be inefficient, bureaucratic, and the cause of distortions and waste throughout the economy—not just wasteful, but made up of pure waste and the drag of incalculability. The above considerations, explored and developed into a branch of (post-) Austrian economic theory called "democratic process theory," might reveal that the public conversation and cooperation of the population through this nonmarket spontaneous order has the potential to be just as important and innovative as the market, so long as it is given the same freedom that Austrians would like the market to have—with both keeping the other in check, like two sides of a ying-yang, each with its separate sphere, yet each affecting the other. Just as each of us have rights that limit the rights of the other (so that they have no right to harm us), the need for the market to exist must limit the democratic sphere and the need for the democratic sphere to exist must limit the market.

CONCLUSION

Democracy, just like the market, is a process and an order; both are made up of people interacting in a spontaneous order consisting of formal and informal institutions inside of which the individual acts, reacts, and interacts. The people work within society, and react to it, rather than merely taking isolated action, as is assumed by a model based on individualism and individual preferences. The democratic process is also a spontaneous order with the potential to be as evolutionary and dynamic as the market process, and it too is based upon interacting individuals, with the capability of cooperation as well as self-interested action. Expectations, habits, and culture are endogenous to the system: they emerge from the system itself. Culture affects an individual's "nature," including her habits, preferences, and the way she responds to the incentives of the system. Imposition of a system upon a public may produce rent-seeking, so rent-seeking may be less of a problem in a system that has emerged from the bottom up and coevolved with the culture. Culture and custom may be more important than even legal institutions, so a decentralized, evolving democratic system, with transparency and public conversation integrated and internal to the system and its coevolving culture, may produce far more efficient public programs, and may not need to be laissez-faire to be growth promoting and poverty reducing, even according to Austrian models. The inclusion of a democratic process theory in addition to market process theory may allow Austrians to study this branch of inquiry.

NOTES

1. For example, Austrians frequently speak about culture in something like the following way: "In economic terms, culture is a tool for the self-regulation of behavior, and as such it either lowers or raises the costs of enforcing the rules of the game." Peter Boettke, "The How, The What, and The Why of the 'Culture Matters' Thesis," Cato Unbound, http://www.cato-unbound.org/2006/12/08/peter-j-boettke/how-what-why-culture-matters-thesis
2. Marx argues that with common property, man would transcend "human self-estrangement" and hence would resolve the dichotomy of the division of self and other, and he predicted "the genuine resolution of the conflict between man and nature and between man and man" (1844: 3rd section, part 2). Based on Marx's theories, and grounded in a philosophy shared by many other socialists, Vladimir Lenin and other Marxist leaders aimed at this kind of unity before and after the revolution. For a particularly well-developed exploration, see Bukharin (2005 [1937]), although it is argued that by then Bukharin was expressing the philosophical framework with irony, as he awaited execution—for exploration of his theories and this argument see Nell (2014a).

   Lenin, and others in the Russian Social-Democratic party, found a simplified blueprint for their ethical ideal in Nikolai Chernyshevsky's novel *What Is to Be Done* (after which Lenin's famous article was named). Lenin's mentor, Georgi Plekhanov, said that, from the novel "we have all drawn moral strength and faith in a better future" (Figes, 1997: 130–131). Chernyshevsky's hero, Rakhmetev, is heroic due to his self-sacrifice and singular purpose: building a society in which the common good is held above all personal pleasures and interests. This was the ideal toward which the revolutionaries in the novel and those reading it worked. Modeling themselves after Rakhmetev was party members' evidence to each other that they were true in their desire to build a new world and new man; it was preparation for the new society that would be built upon this basis (Read, 2005: 12; Figes, 1997: 130–131, 389).

   This was not limited to the Bolsheviks. Marxist E. Belfort Bax (1893) wrote, "At last with the dawn of a new economic era, the era of social production for social uses, we shall have also the dawn of a new Ethic, an Ethic whose ideal is neither personal holiness nor personal interest, but social happiness-for which the perfect individual will ever be subordinate to the perfect society."

Marx (1844) can be found here: https://www.marxists.org/archive/marx/works/1844/manuscripts/comm.htm

Bax (1893) can be found here: https://www.marxists.org/archive/bax/1893/ethics/index.htm

3. Of course, if the society itself is valued very highly, above some alternative society that does not require those tools, then these tools *are* highly valued.
4. Although Hayek did argue that reason developed from market exchange, which is arguably a concession to a historicist position (Nell, 2013).
5. I thank Andy Denis for this concise description of this passage.
6. Shackle, working in tradition with Lachmann, is an exception to this. Shackle takes more seriously than probably any other economist of recent times the uncertainty that time introduces. For example, he writes, "Reason unfolds the meaning of premises. It can do no more. But if one of the premises should be: There are things un-thought of, that time in its operation will suggest, what can reason tell us about that entirety, which contains both the visible premises and the unknown things? . . . Reason and time seem to be at odds, for reason is asked for the meaning of premises always partly unstated" (1972: 25).
7. Austrians also, unhelpfully, explain away nonselfish (altruistic) behavior as self-interested, by redefining preferences to accommodate it.
8. Just like bees and the flowers they pollinate, the individual and society are dependent upon each other, and their interaction helps pass along information and spread the individual's unique contributions (ideas, genes, etc.) far and wide so that they may come into contact with others in the society, and in so doing facilitate evolution, transformation, reproduction, and growth.
9. Austrians have written extensively on this subject. Mises roots all economic activity in "human action," which represents their microfoundations, without which no macroeconomic variable would be able to affect any other. Market process theory, based on Hayekian theory and developed by Israel Kirzner, represents the Austrian model of how individual action produces the macroeconomic outcome of market coordination. Finally, in a six minute video on "what distinguishes Austrian economics," Lachmann includes the issue (Recorded: October 25, 1977, at the department of Economics of the University of Colorado: https://www.youtube.com/watch?v=2xyhKsUseGc).
10. GusdiZerega.com, "What Libertarians Can Add to American Life if They Take the Time to Understand Their Principles," http://dizerega.com/2013/04/24/what-libertarians-can-add-to-american-life-if-they-take-the-time-to-understand-their-principles/.
11. Rational choice theory argues that individuals will shirk because doing so will not affect the outcome enough to have an impact on their own portion

of the total "pie." For example, if taxes were voluntary and an individual chose not to pay her portion, then even if she expected to receive welfare benefits she would calculate that she would be better off if she did not pay because her choice to not pay taxes would only reduce the total revenues by a tiny amount and so would not affect her welfare benefits by a noticeable amount. Rational choice also predicts that individuals will not vote because a single vote is unlikely to change the outcome of an election, even a local one, yet 60–70 percent of eligible voters in most democratic countries do vote, even in nationwide elections in which a single vote is least likely to affect the outcome.

12. Hayek (1944) includes probably the first, or at least most famous, argument of this sort, in his 1944 book *The Road to Serfdom*, which might be seen as a "warning" (or dystopian analysis). In it he presents the road by which Britain could end up as a highly concentrated peacetime war-socialist economy and society, similar to a fascist or Stalinist one: once a certain core part of the economy was run by planners, the rest would inevitably follow, and society would be dragged along with it.

    Nell (2012) relates the collapse of the planned economy into rent-seeking (in Russia) with the consolidation of a market economy, making the case that a rent-seeking unstable equilibrium is reached in both cases—they are merely two sides of the same coin.

13. In this, according to Stringham and Miles (in Nell, 2014c), Austrians are in agreement with David Hume and with new institutional economists, but not with Anthony de Jasay, who saw constraining the state as largely futile.

14. This was one argument for why rational planning should replace competition by various interests—and it was the argument of Austrians that as spontaneous orders lead to knowledge discovery, replacement of them by planning would not be effective.

15. Barbara Wootton (1935) took for granted that collective decision-making (for example, for central planning, but the same would apply to public programs within a mixed economy) only works well if personal and sectional interests (self-interest) are subordinated to the interests of the whole society. In her book, *Plan or No Plan*, Wootton writes of the "peculiarities of the peasant mentality," and the related problem that "factory labour of to-day is recruited from the peasant of yesterday," explaining that for the peasant, the resources "are the property of the persons (and even in collective farms of groups of persons) who are directly interested in the sale of these products." The problem with this is that "The cooperation of these persons can indeed be won on certain terms, but the price of its winning is that the sectional interests of these persons should make their mark on the very content of the plan itself" (1935: 322).

16. "Networks," as a mechanism or mode of coordination, "differ from horizontally coordinated markets as well as from vertically coordinated hierarchies," a recent encyclopedia of public policy reads. "Their actors are

loosely joined in long-term relationships that coincide with the attributes of reciprocity and trust, ensuring cooperation in repeated exchange procedures. Thus, they combine the exchange rationale of markets with the cooperative rationale of hierarchical organizations" (Powell 1990). On this point, see Per Bylund's chapter in Nell (2014c), the first volume of this informal series, which focuses on *Austrian Theory and Economic Organization*. Bylund makes the case that firms need not be hierarchical because they can simply be a nexus of horizontal relationships, acting as networks rather than hierarchies. Can democracies also act as networks, transmitting information and coordinating decision-making laterally? The encyclopedia entry continues: "This reading of institutional networks as a specific mode of governing the interaction of diverse actors resembles the thesis that norms of reciprocity and trust facilitate solutions for the appropriation of common-pool resources that differ markedly from those solutions that favour an exclusive role of private property or government interventions (Ostrom 1990: 211–212)" (Ebner, 2009: 225, available at http://pohara.homestead.com/Encyclopedia/Volume-3.pdf).

REFERENCES

Angner, Erik. 2002. "The History of Hayek's Theory of Cultural Evolution." *Studies in History and Philosophy of Science Part C: Studies in History and Philosophy of Biological and Biomedical Sciences,* 33(4): 695–718.

Bax, E. Belfort. 1893. *The Ethics of Socialism.* London & New York: Swan Sonnenschein. Available at https://www.marxists.org/archive/bax/1893/ethics/index.htm.

Boettke, Peter J., Christopher J. Coyne, and Peter T. Leeson. 2008. "Institutional Stickiness and the New Development Economics." *American Journal of Economics and Sociology,* 67(2): 331–358.

Boettke, Peter J. and Edward J. López. 2002. "Austrian Economics and Public Choice." *The Review of Austrian Economics,* 15(2–3): 111–119.

Bohman, James. 2006. "Deliberative Democracy and the Epistemic Benefits of Diversity." *Episteme: A Journal of Social Epistemology,* 3(3): 175–191.

Buchanan, James M. 1982. "Order Defined in the Process of Its Emergence." *Literature of Liberty,* 5(4): 5–18.

Bukharin, Nikolai. 2005 [1937]. *Philosophical Arabesques.* New York: Monthly Review Press.

Coyne, Christopher J. 2008. *After War: The Political Economy of Exporting Democracy.* Stanford, CA: Stanford University Press.

Crampton, Eric. 2013. "Culture and Agents," *Offsetting Behavior,* April 4, http://offsettingbehaviour.blogspot.co.uk/2013/04/culture-and-agents.html.

Dahlsten, Ulf. 2010. *Market Economy, Democracy and Human Nature.* London: London School of Economics.

diZerega, Gus. 2011. "Spontaneous Order and Liberalism's Complex Relationship to Democracy." *The Independent Review*, 16(2), pp. 173–197. Available at http://www.independent.org/pdf/tir/tir_16_02_2_dizerega.pdf

Ebner, Alexander. 2009. "Governance, Institutions and Collective Action." In Phillip Anthony O'Hara (ed.), *International Encyclopedia of Public Policy Governance in a Global Age, Volume 3: Public Policy and Political Economy*, pp. 218–231. GPERU: Perth. Available at http://pohara.homestead.com/Encyclopedia/Volume-3.pdf

Feldmann, Horst. 2005. "Hayek's Theory of Cultural Evolution: A Critique of the Critiques." In Jürgen G. Backhaus (ed.), *Entrepreneurship, Money And Coordination: Hayek's Theory of Cultural Evolution*, pp. 1–46. Cheltenham: Edward Elgar.

Figes, Orlando. 1997. *A People's Tragedy: A History of the Russian Revolution 1891–1924.* New York: Penguin.

Gagnon, Jean-Paul. 2014. "Democratic Theorists in Conversation: Turns in Contemporary Thought." Available at http://www.palgraveconnect.com/pc/doifinder/10.1057/9781137322777.

Gertz, Nolen. 2009. "What's Wrong with the Torturer?" Available at SSRN: http://ssrn.com/abstract=1399115.

Gick, Evelyn and Wolfgang Gick. 2000. Working paper, "Hayek's Theory of Cultural Evolution Revisited: Rules, Morality, and the Sensory Order," Discussion paper #01/00, Series B (Economics), University of Jena, Department of Economics and Business Administration.

Graeber, David. 2004. *Fragments of an Anarchist Anthropology*. Chicago: Prickly Paradigm Press.

Hayek, F. A. 2002 [1968]. "Competition as a Discovery Procedure." *The Quarterly Journal of Austrian Economics* 5(3): 9–23.

———. 1979. *Law, Legislation, and Liberty, Volume III: The Political Order of a Free People*. Chicago: The University of Chicago Press.

———. 1960. *The Constitution of Liberty*. Chicago: University of Chicago Press.

———. 1945. "The Use of Knowledge in Society." *American Economic Review*, 34(4): 519–530.

———, ed. 1935. *Collectivist Economic Planning: Critical Studies on the Possibilities of Socialism*. London: Routledge & Kegan Paul.

Hilton, Marjorie L. 2004. "Retailing the Revolution: The State Department Store (GUM) and Soviet Society in the 1920s." *Journal of Social History*, 37(4): 939–964.

Horwitz, Steven. 1998. "Monetary Calculation and Mises's Critique of Planning." *History of Political Economy*, 30(3): 427–450.

Ikeda, Sanford. 1990. "Market-Process Theory and 'Dynamic' Theories of the Market." *Southern Economic Journal*, 57(1): 75–92.

Kiaer, Christina and Eric Naiman, eds. 2005. *Everyday Life in Early Soviet Russia.* Bloomington, IN: Indiana University Press.

Krueger, A. 1974. "The Political Economy of a Rent- Seeking Society." *American Economic Review*, 64(3): 291–303.

La Boétie, Estienne de. 1942 [1576]. "The Discourse of Voluntary Servitude" (trans. Harry Kurz). Available at http://oll.libertyfund.org/?option=com_staticxt&staticfile=show.php%3Ftitle=2250&Itemid=27.

Lachmann, Ludwig. 1978. *Capital, Expectations, and the Market Process: Essays on the Theory of the Market Economy.* Kansas City: Sheed and Ward.

———. 1973. *Macro-economic Thinking and the Market Economy: An Essay on the Neglect of the Micro-Foundations and Its Consequences.* London: The Institute of Economic Affairs.

———. 1970. *The Legacy of Max Weber.* London: Heinemann.

Lewin, Peter. 2013. "Hayek and Lachmann and the Complexity of Capital." In Roger Garrison (ed.), *The Elgar Companion to Hayek*, 165–194. Cheltenham: Edward Elgar.

Lenin, Vladimir. 1919. Eighth Congress of the R.C.P.(B.). March 18–23, http://www.marxists.org/archive/lenin/works/1919/rcp8th/03.htm.

Marx, Karl. 1959 [1844]. *Economic and Philosophic Manuscripts of 1844.* Moscow: Progress Publishers.

McCann, J. R. and C. R. McCann Jr. 2002. "F. A. Hayek: The Liberal as Communitarian." *The Review of Austrian Economics*, 15(1): 5–34.

Meisner, Mitch. 1972. "The Shenyang Transformer Factory—A Profile." *The China Quarterly*, 52: 717–737.

Menger, Carl. [1871] 2007. *Principles of Economics.* Auburn, AL: Ludwig von Mises Institute.

Merquior, J. G. 1991. "Death to *Homo Economicus*." *Critical Review*, 5(3): 353–378.

Meyer, David. 2012. "How the German Pirate Party's 'Liquid Democracy' Works." TechPresident.com.

Mises, Ludwig von. [1949] 1996. *Human Action: A Treatise on Economics*, 4th revised ed. San Francisco: Fox & Wilkes.

———. 1935. *Collectivist Economic Planning: Critical Studies on the Possibilities of Socialism.* London: George Routledge & Sons.

Murray, Cameron. 2014. "Micro-foundations Don't Escape Lucas Critique," http://ckmurray.blogspot.com.au/2014/05/micro-foundations-doesnt-solve-lucas.html.

———. 2013. "MacroBusiness, Rumplestatskin, Featured Article in Economics," http://www.macrobusiness.com.au/2013/04/when-culture-is-the-best-explanation/.

Nell, Guinevere Liberty, ed. 2014a. *Spontaneous Order and the Utopian Collective.* New York: Palgrave Macmillan.

———. 2014b. "The Alchemy of the Can Opener: How an Austrian Economist Found Himself Supporting Dictatorial Imposition of a Liberal Order." *Review of Political Economy*, 26(3).

———, ed. 2014c. *Austrian Theory and Economic Organization.* New York: Palgrave Macmillan.

———. 2013. "Welfare in the Austrian Marketplace: Bridging Austrian and Market Socialist Economics." In Guinevere L. Nell (ed.), *Basic Income and the*

Free Market: Austrian Economics and the Potential for Efficient Redistribution, pp. 7–48. New York: Palgrave Macmillan.

———. 2011. "Rent-Seeking, Hierarchy and the Centralization: Why the Soviet Union Collapsed So Fast and What It Means for Market Economies." *Comparative Economic Studies*, 53(4): 593–620.

Ostrom, Elinor. 1990. *Governing the Commons: The Evolution of Institutions for Collective Action*. Cambridge, UK: Cambridge University Press.

Pasour E. C. Jr. 1987. "Rent Seeking: Some Conceptual Problems and Implications." *The Review of Austrian Economics*, 1(1): 123–143.

Read, Christopher. 2005. *Lenin: A Revolutionary Life*. London and New York: Routledge.

Roche, George. 1994. "The Road to Freedom." In Can *Capitalism Cope? Free Market Reform in the Post-Communist World*. Hillsdale, MI: Hillsdale College Press.

Seel, Richard. 2000. "Culture and Complexity: New Insights on Organisational Change." *Organisations & People* 7(2): 2–9. Available at http://www.new-paradigm.co.uk/culture-complex.htm.

Salerno, Joseph T. 1993. "Mises and Hayek Dehomogenized." *The Review of Austrian Economics*, 6(2): 113–146.

Sawyer, R. Keith. 2005. *Social Emergence: Societies as Complex Systems*. Cambridge: Cambridge University Press.

Schlesinger, Rudolf. 1945. *Soviet Legal Theory: Its Social Background and Development*. Oxford: Oxford University Press.

Shackle, G. 1972. *Epistemics and Economics*. Cambridge: Cambridge University Press.

Smith, Adam. 1790 [1759]. *The Theory of Moral Sentiments*. London: A. Millar. Available at http://www.econlib.org/library/Smith/smMS.html.

Stalin, Joseph. 1928. "Against Vulgarising the Slogan of Self-Criticism." In *Works*, Vol. 11, January 1928 to March 1929. Moscow: Foreign Languages Publishing House, 1954. Available at http://www.marxists.org/reference/archive/stalin/works/1928/06/26.htm

Stigler, George J. and Gary S. Becker. 1977. "De Gustibus Non Est Disputandum." *The American Economic Review*, 67(2): 76–90.

Tullock, Gordon. 2005. "18. The Case against the Common Law." In Francesco Parisi and Charles K. Rowley (eds.), *The Origins of Law and Economics: Essays by the Founding Fathers*, 464–474. Cheltenham, UK: Edward Elgar.

Vaughn, Karen. 1994. *Austrian Economics in America*. Cambridge: Cambridge University Press.

Waters, William R. 1998. "Social Economics: A Solidarist Perspective." In *Why Economists Disagree*, New York: State University of New York Press.

Wildevsky, Aaron. 1991. "Can Norms Rescue Self-Interest or Macro Explanation Be Joined to Micro?" *Critical Review*, 5(3): 301–323

Yunker, James, A. 2001. *On the Political Economy of Market Socialism: Essays and Analyses*. Alternative Voices in Contemporary Economics series. Aldershot: Ashgate.

Zwolinski, Matthew. 2008. "The Separateness of Persons and Liberal Theory." *Journal of Value Inquiry*, 42(2): 147–165.

Zywicki, Todd J. 2007. "Gordon Tullock's Critique of the Common Law." George Mason Law & Economics Research Paper No. 07-13. Available at SSRN: http://ssrn.com/abstract=964781.

CHAPTER 4

On the Varieties of Spontaneous Orders: From Cultures to Civil Societies and the Orders In Between

Troy Camplin

Introduction

Human beings are social animals. Specifically, we are a species of social ape, which evolved from the social primates, which are a kind of social mammal. And most mammals are social. Human beings, however, appear to be the most social mammal of all. Our sociality is so strong that we are able to live in considerable peace in cities containing millions of people, countries containing up to over a billion people, and a world of around seven billion. We know of each other's existences and rarely engage in raids or battles. In this, we are completely different from our nearest relatives, the chimpanzees, who would immediately engage in genocide of any other group about whom they came to know. As Frans de Waal has observed, ten million chimpanzees in a city would create a bloodbath unlike anything ever seen committed by human beings (Querna, 2005).

The social sciences—even those most dedicated to an individualistic worldview—all recognize that humans are social. This, however, is not at all in conflict with human individuality. If anything, it is precisely our sociality that drives our individualism, and our individualism that keeps our societies dynamic. Without these tensions, we would not see social dynamism, but social stagnation and mass psychology.

In this chapter I want to investigate how human beings in their interactions give rise to a variety of social spontaneous orders. Humans live in cultures, a variety of spontaneous orders, and in civil society. These networks emerge from the bottom-up, and are a result of human action and are not of human design. In some places, where there are homogeneous populations, these divisions are difficult to make. But in more heterogeneous populations, we see ever greater divisions. Heterogeneous civil societies like the United States contain within them a large number of social spontaneous orders, from science to technology to trade, and a variety of cultures. The cultures affect the spontaneous orders locally, and the spontaneous orders and cultures interact to create civil societies. Changes in any of these affect the others in very complex ways. This complexity is why it is important to understand the parts and how those parts interact, all of which has an effect on how the individuals within civil society act and interact and, thus, affect the structures of those orders.

With the understanding that all of these orders in fact start with interacting individuals, I will begin with a brief section on culture, followed by a discussion of Frederick Turner's idea of multiple economies. Building on the work of Turner, I will propose a set of spontaneous orders and discuss how they relate to each other, the consequences of those relations to each other, the content of culture, and the individuals participating in these social networks. I will then end with a discussion of how this all comes together to form civil society.

CULTURE

Culture is "the transfer of information by behavioral means, most particularly by the process of teaching and learning. . . . The information passed on in a cultural fashion accumulates in the form of knowledge and tradition" (Bonner, 1980: 9). As a result, "Culture is a whole orientation to the world, a way of living that necessarily involves ethical choices" (Lavoie and Chamlee-Wright, 2000: 12). This perspective agrees with Ruth Benedict's understanding of culture (1934). I shall be drawing upon her work in no small part because she views cultures as spontaneous orders. Given this definition, one could easily argue that the practice of trade is a "form of knowledge and tradition," a ritual and a custom that has been passed down through the generations, and thus is properly understood as part of culture. Indeed. Certainly the particular ways in which we engage in this or that social activity are properly understood as being part of culture. Whether one walks to the open air market every third day or drives to the big box grocery store is in no small part a reflection of one's culture. But people's engaging in trade is a cultural universal. It occurs under natural, peaceful conditions, and requires active force to squelch (and even then, black markets always emerge). That is, if you have two people, each of whom wants something the other has more than they want what they themselves have, mutual trade between the two will naturally emerge (so long as each wants to benefit from the other in the future). The act of trade itself can be isolated from other aspects of culture and analyzed—those who do so are called economists. And the act of trade can also develop on its own, independent from a particular culture. A good example of this would be trade within the United States. There are a large number of cultures and subcultures within the United States, but the ways in which we engage in trade are highly similar and thus cut across these (sub)cultures. But in each case, we still have to come back to the fact that the particular aspects of who is trading involves cultural—indeed, moral—decisions.

Benedict argues that cultures develop their own personalities, from the dominant personalities of the individuals within those cultures. One result is the development of quite different definitions of who fits in and who is a social outcast. This can be a significant problem for those whose temperaments do not allow them to fit in well with the culture into which they were born, when their culture is separated from other cultures by the xenophobia inherent in tribalism. One of the benefits of what F. A. Hayek calls the Great Society is that it manages to hold together a wide number of heterogeneous groups, allowing for peaceful movement among those groups, and thus allowing those who do not fit in with the group into which they were born to find another group with which they feel more at home, or to even form their own group. The Great Society is the solution to what Mark Pagel (2012) notes constitutes the paradox of human existence: "our unmatched ability to get along with each other set against our tendencies to form competing societies often not far from conflict" (x). Competition and cooperation are the two main drivers of both our diversification and our unity. And, as we will see, a major driver of the development of the Great Society is the emergence of independent, often cooperative, but equally often competitive, social spontaneous orders.

Given that different cultures develop their own personalities from our evolved psychological tendencies (a process modeled by Kenrick et al., 2002; 2003), it is perhaps not surprising to learn that some cultures are more conducive to the full development and smooth workings of complex spontaneous orders than are others. Martin and Storr (2008) argue that perverse spontaneous orders can emerge. They identify two kinds:

mobs and cultures that discourage work, thrift, and diversity. Indeed, their implicit argument that homogeneity in a culture is fundamentally perverse is supported by Sobel et al. (2010), who demonstrate that, in the United States, which has very similar economic institutions across the country, entrepreneurial activity and economic growth are positively correlated with heterogeneity. Poorer states, like West Virginia, are much more homogeneous than are wealthier states, like Texas. The presence of heterogeneous populations, of a wide variety of cultures within a relatively small geographical location, perhaps in turn drives the emergence of spontaneous orders precisely because such orders are impersonal, meaning they make interactions among very different people and peoples easier and, thus, more likely.

All of this suggests that the details of any given culture may come into conflict with some particular social spontaneous order, and the values of that order. Further, the values promoted by each spontaneous order, and the products of each order, in turn affect the content of culture. This can be most clearly seen when we understand that all of our social spontaneous orders are in fact kinds of institutions. As Robert Wuthnow argues, when we study culture, we

> must pay attention to speakers and audiences, discursive texts, the rituals in which discourse is embedded, and the social contexts in which it is produced. As something that is not simply affirmed subjectively but produced collectively, culture clearly depends on social resources, and the availability and distribution of these resources is likely to play a major role in influencing the direction of cultural change. Cultural change necessitates, even more so than before, an approach that focuses on the institutional contexts in which it is produced, enacted, disseminated, and altered. (1992: 274)

These institutional contexts are the different spontaneous orders that emerge and the organizations we create. Wuthnow thus argues that we should consider the products of the spontaneous orders of the arts to be the very contents of culture—a position hardly controversial. However, Hayek helps us understand that this is but part of it. In addition, we see another relationship between the artistic order and culture (indeed, between any given order and a culture), when he identifies culture as a result of "spillover effects," or unintended consequences:

> It does not make sense to apply the standards of conscious conduct to those unintended consequences of individual action which all the truly social represents, except by eliminating the unintended—which would mean eliminating all that we call culture. (Hayek, 1973: 33)

Culture is what one gets from both the products and the effects of art and literature, religion, philosophy, and so forth, which in turn affects each of the spontaneous orders. One must be careful, then, neither to praise the culture over the order(s) in question nor blame the culture for being incompatible with whatever order we are interested in understanding (or, for the more politically minded, promote). Any given culture, too, is an emergent order, and it grows and changes in negotiation with past customs, with the entire history of that culture. Cultures are always in a state of evolution, and contact with other cultures and other orders creates the conditions for more rapid cultural change than might have otherwise occurred. We see this occurring around the world. The important thing is, if one is an outsider, to allow that change to take place on its own time and neither to force things nor impose one's own values on the culture.

At the same time, culture matters a great deal when it comes to how successful any given spontaneous order is going to be. Lavoie and Chamlee-Wright note that economic prosperity "depends as much upon a certain 'enterprising spirit,' a set of values, attitudes, aspirations, and orientations in the culture, as it does upon any so-called objective or material conditions of the society" and that "The question of how culture may be more or less conducive to economic prosperity is too culture-specific to be usefully answered in the abstract, and at the coarse aggregative level of national GDP comparisons" (2000: 11). At the same time, McCloskey (2006) observes that one of the most important factors leading to the rapid takeoff of the catallaxy in the West and the resultant creation of widespread wealth was a specific change in the culture—the rhetoric surrounding business. As attitudes toward business, profit, and innovation changed, becoming more and more supportive of such endeavors, the catallaxy developed more and more and became more and more distinct from other social orders. Whether one sees business as inherently moral or immoral, worth pursuing or avoiding, will make a huge difference in its structure and, consequently, in what people do within it and how wealth is created and distributed within it.

These cultural elements can even have quite long-term effects. The continued dominance of Jews in banking in the West stems from the medieval prohibitions on Christians lending each other money at interest (Mercer, 2010). This prohibition, as well as anti-Semitic attitudes (also cultural) that prevented many Christians from borrowing money from the only group that could do so at interest and thus would in fact lend money, was likely a major contributing factor to the ongoing economic stagnation of the time. As these cultural attitudes changed, economic behaviors changed, and as economic behaviors changed and people started becoming wealthy, people started emulating those who were economically successful, resulting in a change in culture. Eventually, Christians wanted in on the usury game, so they too could make money, and this in turn led to changes in the law. The original laws were, of course, put in place by people who saw themselves as following the will of God and His Church, so the law itself was reflective of the culture of the time. But economic changes led to cultural changes, which led to legal changes and, thus, to more economic changes. And so on. The result was a move from the medieval world into the Renaissance and mercantilism and, eventually, into modernism and capitalism. An independent economic order thus emerged out of an order in which economy, governance, and religion were difficult at best to untangle.

All of this also suggests that it is difficult to untangle cause and effect. Are sex and racial discrimination economic problems? Or are they cultural problems? One would expect a racist or sexist culture to have that racism or sexism expressed in the business practices of those participating in the economy of that culture. The racism or sexism is not caused by the economic order, but by the culture underlying that order. Laws, too, are typically going to be an expression of the culture—which explains why states in the American South had many racist laws on their books prior to the 1964 Civil Rights Act passed by the federal government to overturn those laws. It is interesting to note that many of the laws on the books expressly prohibited certain interracial economic exchanges from taking place. The presence of the laws suggests that, without the force of law, whites would have hired and/or served African Americans, in violation of the prevailing cultural norms. As a result, the political order prevented the economic order from changing the prevailing culture. So while it is true that business practices can be traced to cultural attitudes, cultural attitudes can equally be changed through business practices. A racist person who hires someone of another race because it is cheaper to do so—and because they are more greedy than racist—will then have to interact with that person he or she hired, meaning he/she will come to actually know that individual as a person after a while. It is difficult to maintain hatreds like racism once you actually know a person of another race, meaning that hiring and working alongside people of other races will result in less racism over time. The fact that racist laws specifically targeted these economic interactions is telling.

Thus the economy can provide any number of solutions to what many would perceive as cultural ills. However, as the above discussion suggests, we are talking about a complex process that is going to unfold over time—a process that can be blocked by other processes, such as those that come out of other orders. The political order is fundamentally conservative in nature—those acting within it are typically seeking ways to "stabilize" other orders, be they economic orders (for the Left) or cultural orders (for the Right)—while most of the other orders are transformative. Even "revolutionary" politics such as the Communist revolution came about to create greater stability and predictability. That is the purpose, after all, behind economic planning—to eliminate the chaotic elements of the free market. Karl Marx argues that man in his natural, tribal state was communist. Regardless of the kind, revolutionaries all promise temporary change now to create a stable social order in the future. It is this desire for long-term stability and lack of change that I am calling "conservative." Moreover, political conflicts that result in what appears to be radical change are really a conflict between two already established political ideologies. The apparent radicalism of the 1960s in the promotion of civil rights was really a demand that "all men are created equal"—an American political ideal almost two hundred years old by the 1960s—be in fact realized. What is more, it was an importation from the moral order into the political order, temporarily radicalizing the latter. Culture, being rooted in traditions, is also fundamentally conservative. It changes but slowly—although this is not necessarily a condemnation of it (or of the equally conservative political order). Although for the longest time anthropologists believed "traditional" cultures did not change over long periods of time, they have come to realize that quite the opposite is true. All cultures change over time—sometimes slowly, sometimes rapidly, but always in the context of tradition, of what came before. As Hayek (1960) observed, this is precisely how healthy growth in a social order occurs.

My emphasis on the interactions of the economy with culture should not, however, lead one to believe that the market economy and its spontaneous orders are necessarily the most important for us in understanding civil society. If I focus a little more on the interactions between the market economy and the other economies and orders, it is because I am aware my audience is mostly economists. Further, as we will see, many of the spontaneous orders I will be discussing involve what we have typically considered "cultural creations"—art, literature, religion, philosophy, and so on. We will see, however, that in many cases what is happening in each of these "cultural" orders involves a few people at the most conspicuous levels (a fact not atypical of any spontaneous order), and that these big players influence the broader culture both directly and indirectly, and often in forms within the popular culture that are barely recognizable by the originator of the idea. Thus, we will not be abandoning the discussion of culture as we take up the discussion of economies and spontaneous orders; rather, we will continue the discussion of culture in a more analytical fashion, looking at several of its parts in turn.

On the Varieties of Economies

Frederick Turner (2005) argues that civil society is divided into different kinds of economies: divine, market, political, and gift. Turner also includes the environmental economy, by which he means the biosphere and its various biomes and ecosystems. In fact, we can see a clear parallel between civil society and the biosphere, with Turner's economies finding their ecological equivalents in the biomes and the various spontaneous orders in the various ecosystems. The local physical environment can in fact have significant effects on the contents of our cultures—Gad Saad (2011) gives the example of spicy foods (and especially spicy meat dishes) being most popular in hotter climates, because spices can cover the taste of slightly spoiled meat (perhaps not coincidentally, hot peppers also have antibacterial properties)—so we should not too quickly dismiss the importance of the environmental economy, of which humans are necessarily a part.

Although one can draw definite parallels between biomes and the human economies Turner lists, such as the necessary presence of heterogeneity, scale-free networks, and evolution, we will leave aside the environmental economy to focus on the different human economies. The market economy is the one we are most likely to attribute to being an economy, yet Turner makes a good case for the others being kinds of economies as well—especially when we consider "economy" in its original, Greek, sense as the rules of the household. That household was once literal, but has, through its more recent usage, become associated with a much larger household of many more (and unrelated) members. The rules of this larger household, however, are quite different from the rules of an actual household. A self-organizing, scale-free network process has very different rules and a very different structure from a created hierarchical organization network. Many of our social ills come about precisely because we confuse the two—a confusion rooted in the Greek term "economy." Nevertheless, we are faced with the fact that the term economy is not going to return to its original meaning—and with the fact that if we follow Turner's divisions, we are in fact expanding the term in the opposite direction, as Turner's economies are themselves made up of subsets of interacting spontaneous orders. Indeed, Turner argues that we can understand gift-giving, religious interactions, and political interactions as kinds of economies. The important thing in each case is that there are different kinds of interactions, resulting in different kinds of economies with different kinds of outcomes.

For example, in the market economy, each person is seeking to increase profit through mutual trade. You are successful in the market economy insofar as you create profit. Wealth is measured in money; information is communicated in prices. In the gift economy, however, your intention is to bestow gifts on others, thus promoting the good, the true, and the beautiful. That gift may be money, the creation of scientific knowledge, the creation of a work of art, and so forth. The gift economy worker will do that work even if they are not paid to do so. Moreover, they will typically spend their own resources in order to create within the gift economy. As a result, one's success in the gift economy is not measured by profit, but by reputation. The divine economy promotes morality and is measured by sacrifice. This brings us to the political economy, which promotes justice and, when the political economy becomes a democratic order, community values, and is measured by power (or votes, in the democratic order).

Of course, Turner's divisions are hardly the only ones possible. Kenneth Boulding (1985) also argues we create different social systems, with social cooperation resulting in an "exchange system" and social competition resulting in a "threat system." There is also an "integrative system," containing organizations like churches, monasteries, religious organizations, families and clubs (83–89). Artists would belong to the "integrative system" in Boulding's formulation and to the gift economy in Turner's. However, Turner further divides the integrative system into the divine and the gift economies, recognizing each as having different kinds of exchange and producing different kinds of outcomes and social relations. While these are good as far as they go, I would continue to divide these economies further, into different kinds of spontaneous social orders.

ON THE VARIETIES OF SPONTANEOUS ORDERS

Each of the social systems discussed in this chapter is a kind of network. But spontaneous orders are a certain kind of network. Gus diZerega observes that there are "Certain common qualities [that] are unique to *all* spontaneous orders. Their rules have to be *procedural*, facilitate *cooperation*, and in a formal sense apply to all *equally*" (2013: 11 emphasis in original). There is also freedom of entry and exit, organizations to facilitate individual goals, and particular products (prices in the catallaxy, new physical products in the technological orders, artistic products in the artistic order[s], etc.). This means that

> Participants are equal in status and all are equally subject to whatever rules must be followed to participate within the order. All are free to apply these rules to any project of their choosing. Anything that can be pursued without violating a rule is permitted, including pursuing mutually contradictory

goals. Finally, these rules facilitate cooperation among strangers based on certain broadly shared values that are simpler than the values actually motivating many people when they participate. (diZerega, 2013: 9)

This latter is an important point. While each individual has his or her values—and own particular value rankings—there are also systemic values, which are "values privileged by the order itself, values that strengthen as orders develop" (diZerega, 2013: 10). This means that the values privileged by any given system may come into conflict with the values of any given individual at any given time—but perhaps not at other times, or for other people. Opponents of markets, for example, often oppose markets because they see their own values in conflict with those privileged by the market. On the other hand, too many proponents of the free market act as though market-privileged values are the only ones—or the only ones that matter. I would propose to both market opponents and proponents that just because others do not share your values, that does not mean those values are less worthwhile than are your own. Unless you are open to the fact that values and value rankings other than your own are valid, you will not be open to understanding the value of differing values, and thus you will not be open to understanding the value (and values) of each of the spontaneous orders.

While there is a variety of spontaneous orders, including language and morals, I want to concentrate on only a few—which happen to be very closely related to each other. diZerega himself notes some similarities among several spontaneous orders when he argues that "democracy, science, the market, and the web can be considered as specialized

	Abstract	**Mixed**	**Concrete**
Pure Knowledge	Mathematics (gift)	Science (gift)	Science Technology (gift)
Practical Knowledge	Money/Finance (market)	Catallaxy (market)	Market Technology (market)
Pure Wisdom	Philosophy (gift/divine)	Religion (divine)	Art and Literature (gift)
Practical Wisdom	Social Sciences (gift)	Democracy (political)	Philanthropy (gift)

Figure 4.1

communicative subsets immersed within language, which itself makes civil society possible" (diZerega, 2013: 13). Indeed, we will see how communication dominates the spontaneous orders. However, I want to point out not just the similarities but also some salient differences. And while there is considerable merit to the divisions of civil society suggested by Turner and Boulding into different economies, I would like to suggest we further divide these economies into their constituent spontaneous orders (keeping in mind that some, such as money/finance, are not as fully developed spontaneous orders as others), as I demonstrate in Figure 4.1.

Each of the spontaneous orders in Figure 1 produces particular outcomes. These outcomes are in many ways different from the intentions of the system participants. In the sciences, each individual scientist is interested in seeking the truth. Yet, "In doing so they rely on methods devised to provide reliable knowledge so that they can demonstrate their findings to others" (diZerega 2013: 7). As a result, the spontaneous orders of math, the natural sciences, and science technology all produce pure (or, reliable) knowledge. People participate in the market for a variety of reasons, but the outcome of the market process is prices, which is a form of knowledge. As Hayek suggested, the catallaxy, or the realm of human economic exchange, produces knowledge through competition. Competition is a discovery procedure. When we make a discovery, we have a new piece of information, meaning we are (potentially) more knowledgeable. In the case of the catallaxy, this knowledge is practical, useful for everyday living. Which is why it is in the realm of practical knowledge production. Technological innovation to create market products is equally knowledge producing in this sense, as is money and finance. Prices and interest rates are ways to provide accurate information about the availability of scarce resources and the values people place on various goods and resources. Price controls, manipulations of money supply and interest rates, and centralized control of resources and innovation all interfere with the production of accurate knowledge (if spontaneous orders could have intentions, we would call them lies). Competition, however, allows for the discovery and transmission of accurate information as knowledge. Naturally, none of these are the reasons anyone participates in the market economy—these are but the consequences of that participation.

Competition is a discovery procedure not only in the catallaxy but in each spontaneous order listed. The outcome of each, however, is going to be different—in no small part because the rules of each order are different. Philosophy produces pure wisdom as individual philosophers try to gain understanding of some system in the world. And as Randall Collins (1998) observes, philosophers are at their most creative when there is active competition. Monopolization (often by using political power) results in stagnation. Thus, when the Catholic monopoly on Christianity was broken in Western Europe, there was a proliferation of new variations on Christianity, resulting in the discovery of new ways to understand not just Christianity but the world in general. And when we have democracy and peacefully competing governments, we can discover the best ways of governing.

If these social orders are spontaneous orders, we would expect them to have many structural similarities, despite the differences in certain details. Understanding these structural similarities—abstract procedural rules, simultaneous positive and negative feedback, status equality among participants—can thus help us understand that what works (or fails to work) in one may very well work (or fail to work) in another. If force and coercion result in intellectual stagnation in philosophy, as Collins demonstrates, then perhaps force and coercion in the catallaxy will have similar results. And if monopoly is bad for a broader base of wealth creation in either the catallaxy or philosophy, then perhaps it is bad in governance as well.

But equally, we need to understand the differences among these spontaneous orders—and how they are related to each other, which means I must justify the divisions I have made.

Let us then begin with perhaps the easiest to justify: the set of Pure Knowledge. There are few who would argue that math and the natural sciences are not pursued for the sake of pure knowledge. Further, technology developed exclusively for scientific discovery is technology created for the pursuit of pure knowledge. In addition, a piece of technology is a concrete entity. There is a physical something there. With math, on the other hand, you have abstract symbols symbolizing abstract ideas. Math is the real of pure abstraction. The natural sciences fall somewhere in-between: we are learning general rules about actual things, using the tools of math and technology. Developments in technology have resulted in many scientific discoveries. Equally, developments in mathematics have resulted in new theories in the natural sciences, which can then in turn be tested with technologies developed to test those theories. We are seeing ideas in quantum physics developed fifty years ago being tested and confirmed with technology that was only recently developed. Note, too, the influences on each. It was developments in new technologies that set off the scientific revolution. It was developments in new mathematical ideas that set off the quantum physics and relativity revolutions within science. Where these orders overlap, we get feedback resulting in the creation of a region where far-from-equilibrium conditions hold and, thus, creativity takes place.

We can see the same basic patterns in the realm of Practical Knowledge. We see technological innovation taking place. With the catallaxy, we have a mixture of, among other things, trade (a concrete activity) and trust (abstract), with increases in trust resulting in more trade, for example. Money symbolizes what we owe others. Prices are the simple feedback signal within the market economy. Hayek (1973) observed that the catallaxy was one of the most developed of the spontaneous orders, but that money and finance was, in fact, one of the least. Part of the reason for this was the political power to be gained in controlling money and finance, meaning governments were rarely going to let there be free banking. A central bank means central planning of money and finance. The arguments against central planning for the catallaxy and technological innovation equally apply to money. In any case, money/finance fall into the realm of abstraction, as a thing is money and has value as money only because humans think it does. The value of money is entirely socially constructed. This is true whether you have a gold (or some other) standard or fiat money, full or fractional reserve banking. It is this recognition that money is abstract that drives arguments against usury (this, and the failure to recognize that you are in fact buying something when you borrow at interest: time). Recognizing the nonneutrality of money means recognizing that money/finance, when it overlaps with the catallaxy, provides powerful feedback. Periods in which positive feedback dominates result in economic bubbles; periods in which negative feedback dominates result in recessions. Given the fact that money/finance has only ever rarely been a spontaneous order (in rare places, for short periods of time), it is difficult to say what a bipolar feedback model of money will in fact look like. However, if the general model holds, we should see greater creativity and greater systemic stability from the system's being more responsive to the overall market economy set of orders (this model seems to be supported by Sabelli, 2005).

Separating the catallaxy from money/finance and market technology can help us see what these processes look like in their purity and the consequences of their interactions. We can also perhaps clear up a few issues within economics as a field. For one, we can see why economists have traditionally considered technology to be an exogenous factor. If the study of economics is only the study of the catallaxy, then technology is of course exogenous (it has its own order). But if the economy in fact consists of three different orders, then economists need to study those orders—separately and together. Joseph Schumpeter viewed technological innovation as being part of the economy, making him a forerunner of this idea. The Schumpeterian entrepreneur is thus one who is in fact working in the overlapping catallactic and technological orders. The Kirznerian entrepreneur is one who is primarily working in the catallaxy (although what he notices may make him decide to become a technological innovator, this is hardly necessary if one is merely engaging in arbitrage). Equally, the Austrian School and monetarist economists view money and finance as important for understanding boom-bust cycles in the catallaxy. An economics that took into consideration both technological innovation and the role of money and finance when analyzing the catallaxy would necessarily be an extremely complex economics—but one much more able to understand the economy as it is.

Knowledge helps us do things, but wisdom helps us understand things, so what we do makes sense in a larger social context. Knowledge cannot bring us wisdom, although it can be a helpful companion to it. This distinction helps us understand why I divided the orders into knowledge and wisdom. And within wisdom, we again see divisions into pure and practical, and abstract, mixed, and concrete.

Just as we pursue knowledge for the sake of knowledge, we pursue wisdom for the sake of wisdom. At its most abstract, we have the realm of philosophy. Randall Collins goes into great detail on the workings of the global philosophical spontaneous order(s). David Andersson (2010) suggests we have seen the emergence of religious spontaneous orders in at least the United States and post-World War II Japan. I have laid the groundwork for understanding artistic and literary production as a spontaneous order. In many ways, these orders are some of the least developed by social scientists, although in many ways they are the most developed in the real world, having been relatively free since ancient times (at least, philosophy and the arts and literature have been). We have also, however, seen places where illiberal governments, such as those of the Soviet Union and Maoist China, have attempted to eliminate these orders as orders and to control artistic, literary, and philosophical output, with the result of there being considerable cultural stagnation. Freeing these orders to become spontaneous orders again, at least to some degree, has in fact resulted in artistic, literary, and philosophical innovation in Russia and China in more recent decades.

Among the wisdom orders, philosophy should be considered the most abstract, dealing as it does in ideas—often with little or no concern for the real world. Religion, on the other hand, is deeply concerned with the real world, and the ramifications of what we do in this world for the world of abstraction (however conceived). Art and literature (see Camplin 2010 on the arts and literature as spontaneous orders), on the other hand, always deal with the physical world, either directly in the use of physical objects, or indirectly in having concrete referents (the worst thing you can do in fiction or poetry is to be completely abstract—you are no longer creating literature, but rather philosophy, when you do so). We of course see any number of overlaps among these orders. Consider all of the religious art, music, poetry, and so on. Consider the philosophers who were also religious figures and leaders. Indeed, one of the most productive times in French literature and philosophy was when philosophy and literature overlapped during the existentialist period. But note that for this to occur, each order must exist as a spontaneous order and be free to interact. When the Soviet Union attempted to impose the philosophy of historical materialism on literature, the result was bland, identical Soviet Realism.

Finally, we come to the realm of Practical Wisdom. One might even call this the moral economy. If we understand it as the moral economy, we can begin to understand why I have placed the orders where I placed them. Philanthropy is a clear example of this, precisely because it is the most concrete. In philanthropy, one is giving one's actual time and/or money to do actual things and to help particular people. Once one of the most developed of orders, philanthropy has in the past century fallen on hard times. In no small part, it has shrunk in size and complexity because many of its roles have been taken over by government. We will discuss this shortly, when we come to the discussion of governance as a spontaneous order.

Perhaps the most controversial division I have made is in separating the social scientists from the natural scientists. This would seem to suggest that social scientists are not "real scientists." In truth, they are not. Social scientists are theorizing and calculating and recommending, but not actually doing anything directly. They are trying to understand processes more complex than themselves, meaning they cannot ever produce the kind of knowledge a natural scientist can produce. Indeed, my placement of the social sciences in the realm of Abstract Practical Wisdom, or the moral economy, shows the wisdom of the older term for the social sciences: the moral sciences. They are and continue to be the moral sciences, which suggests their methodologies should be closer to those used by other wisdom orders, such as philosophy, and less like the far more distant natural sciences. We can thus also see why the use of mathematics made sense in economics—both are abstract orders. However, given my short discussion of the differences between wisdom and knowledge, we can see too why this use has been problematic at best. Wisdom requires a consideration of all of the elements of a system, and math is but one tiny element one should consider.

Finally, we come to the issue of democracy, the spontaneous order form of governance. The purpose of governance is to try to ensure justice within civil society. Any particular government is an organization within the larger democratic spontaneous order (when such an order in fact emerges). A particular government organization can become dominant, but insofar as there is a democratic order, we have in fact a proliferation of far more local, competing areas of governance. The states of the United States were originally conceived of as being competing democratic polities, with freedom of movement of people and goods creating the conditions for competition. Immigration and trade barriers act to protect polities from having to compete, thus establishing and enforcing local monopolies on political power. This political power is used to actually enforce (concrete) various moral codes (abstract). As ideas of justice evolve, so too does the democratic order. This order draws on the discoveries made within the social sciences, and often supports the work of scientists within the social sciences order. This is why few economists really study the economy to understand it rather than to engage in political economy.

The placement of democracy and philanthropy in the practical wisdom economy also helps us understand why democratic governments think they ought to engage in philanthropy. Given the mixed nature of democracy, meaning there are concrete elements to it, it may seem natural to subsume philanthropy into the activities of democracy. Although democracies seek "public values," which diZerega defines as those values that "citizens want manifested within the community as a whole" (2013: 11), if we understand that the only form of justice any government can engage in is vengeance against injustices, we can perhaps see the problem with even democracies engaging in philanthropy. For a government to legitimately engage in philanthropy, the people it is helping have to have experienced some sort of injustice. We see this understanding played out when politicians arguing for a redistribution of wealth talk about the rich getting richer and the poor getting poorer, as though the economy were a zero-sum game, meaning the rich had to have gotten rich by making the poor poorer. This is why governmental redistribution is typically couched in terms of "fairness" and "injustice," meaning that governmental redistribution is in fact understood by politicians as being retribution against those who have "benefited unfairly." Governmental redistribution makes less sense, however, if you realize it is not an injustice against you if someone has made more economic transactions than you have, making them financially wealthier. Yet, as primatological studies have shown, when two individuals are given different pay for the same work, there is a feeling that there has been an injustice. This is the source of envy. The envious feel that their work—which is often of different kinds and values than others'—is worth what others are making and that, therefore, an injustice has been perpetuated. This seems to be particularly strongly felt by many participants in the gift economy, who sometimes forget they are working in the gift economy and not in the market economy, and so should not expect to receive the same financial compensation for their work—which they demonstrate they are willing to do for free and give away as a gift (and why should anyone pay you to do something you are willing to do for free?)—as those working in the market economy. This is further exacerbated by the fact that every so often someone in the gift economy creates something people are willing to pay for, shifting that person much more into the market economy and making the rest wonder why they cannot be so popular. This envy of the success of others often results in complaints that the market makes people have bad taste—meaning any taste other than that held by the gift economy worker. Oftentimes this envy remains as resentment against market outcomes even when the gift economy worker becomes successful in the market economy. Envy is what then drives our use of governments to engage in philanthropy as vengeance against perceived economic injustices.

In describing each of these orders and categories of orders, I have also discussed the consequences of certain overlaps. This does not mean that there are not other potential overlaps. Governmental protection of property rights—and their regulations—affect the structure of the market economy. Some science technologies (nuclear magnetic resonance machines) have become market technologies (MRI machines). Math became very important to the development of philosophy, and vice versa, in the late nineteenth and the early twentieth century in Europe (with Bertrand Russell et al.). The printing press (market technology) had a profound effect on literature, religion, philosophy, governance, the social sciences, science, mathematics, and money (you cannot have fiat money before you have a printing press). The Internet (market technology, beginning as a science technology) is having a similar effect now, and can even be properly understood as its own self-organizing, scale-free network. Russell Berman (2007) argues that literature has an effect on our ideas of individualism and, thus, on the political order. However, to note that there are overlaps is not necessarily to recommend that any order completely overlap any other order. It is one thing to influence and trade; it is another to conquer and colonize. The evils are much the same in our social orders as they are between groups of people—and for the same reason, since our social orders are in fact made of individuals. So while the democratic order might overlap with philanthropy here and there on occasion, with positive results, if it were to completely take over philanthropy, it would destroy it—and perhaps itself—in the process (much as a desert taking over a grassland will destroy the grassland). If the welfare states around the world collapse, this will have been why.

On Civil Society

Civil society is the combination of all of our emergent social orders, including culture and the different spontaneous orders. As a result,

"Unlike spontaneous orders, civil society is not coordinated by any single system of feedback signals, but incorporates many," including all of those of the spontaneous orders. "This abundance of feedback means that no single standard of success or failure is defined within civil society" (diZerega, 2013: 13). Different particular rules of different orders and cultures are going to result in different civil societies.

Each local democratic order is going to create different local laws reflecting those local public values, creating different local civil societies. So too with different institutional settings, different cultures, different populations, and so on. Keep every other order the same and vary only one, and you have a different civil society. This is because when the different orders overlap, they interact in unpredictable ways, giving rise to quite different civil societies. This will be true even if there is an overarching civil society, such as one finds in the United States. Within that larger civil society, we find the civil societies of New York, Kentucky, California, and Texas; within the civil society of Texas, we have that of the Rio Grande Valley, Houston, Austin, and Dallas-Ft. Worth (with some similarities between Dallas-Ft. Worth and Kentucky, as both developed out of Scotch-Irish culture), and so on. Different cultures are going to affect what jobs people think are worth doing (whether they think the work creates value, is below their dignity, etc.), whether or not work is highly valued at all, and so on—all of which affects the catallaxy. The artistic order can become impoverished in a civil society with a culture that influences its members to consider art to be of little value, or can become greatly enriched in a society with a culture that influences its members to consider art to be of the highest value.

As a result, we feel more at home in some civil societies than in others (diZerega, 2013: 14). It may be the one in which we grew up, or it may be one quite different from the one in which we grew up. So long as we have the freedom of entry and exit, we can find our homes, find those who share our values, and join them in their culture and subculture, within those civil societies. This freedom of movement—and the respect for others who have other values we may not share, such that we are willing to allow them to express those values and live in civil societies reflecting those values—is precisely what allows civil societies to be, well, civil. This suggests why it was that people in the Soviet Union became considerably less civil toward each other. Civil society, except among small groups, behind closed doors, as it were, all but disappeared in the Soviet Union precisely because the spontaneous orders had all been collapsed into the massive state hierarchy. As diZerega observes, "civil society constitutes the realm of freedom within society" (2013: 13), meaning without freedom, there can be no civil society. By bringing together all the orders and the values they privilege, civil society is not reducible to the thin values of any one spontaneous order, but rather becomes a realm of thick and overlapping values. But again, reflecting the insights of Benedict, each civil society is going to influence people to rank those values in different ways, making different civil societies attractive to different people—to those whose value rankings are similar to those of others within that particular civil society. Freedom of movement and freedom to develop a wide variety of civil societies are what allow people to find their fits.

If civil society is a self-organizing, scale-free network process made up of a variety of spontaneous orders, this then suggests that civil society, like all complex, scale-free network processes, should exhibit power law distributions. In the same way that the catallaxy will necessarily result in a power law distribution of wealth, with the top 20 percent having 80 percent of the wealth created by the system, we should expect to see power law distributions in each of the spontaneous orders, and in civil society as a whole. We should expect to see a few very large businesses and a large number of small businesses. We should expect to see a few extremely famous artists and a large number of artists about whom nobody will ever hear. We should expect to see a few large churches (like the Catholic Church) and a large number of very small churches (like we find among many Protestant denominations, especially in rural America). And we should expect, in a healthy democracy, to see a lot of small, local polities, and fewer middle-sized polities (such as the states in the U.S.), and even fewer large polities (such as the federal government, to take the U.S. model). This might suggest that power distributions might naturally flow to a few, but the network structures of spontaneous orders complicate this considerably. In scale-free networks, there is considerable fluidity, meaning the 20 percent who own 80 percent of the wealth are not the same people over time. Nor does the wealth of these people in any way prevent the other 80 percent from buying whatever they want with the money they have. However, political power is quite different from wealth. In historical governments, power is a zero sum game; power held by any particular person means it is not held by others. This represents an organizational hierarchy distribution of power, but not a scale-free network distribution of power. In the latter, one would expect each person to in fact have the same political power (in the same way that any person's dollar has the same purchasing power, no matter how wealthy he or she is). What, then, should we expect the results to be? Not a concentration of political power, per se, in the hands of a few; rather, we should expect to see a concentration of political influence in the hands of a few. We would expect the 20 percent with the best political rhetoric to have 80 percent of the persuasive power. They would be able to persuade people to vote in particular ways, but the people would be free to be persuaded or not. Power law distributions allow for the most efficient communication among and movement of people. We should thus expect, if we see a breakdown of power law distributions within a system, to see an unhealthy system—perhaps even one on the verge of collapse, should the power law distributions become too skewed. Knowing all emergent systems have this architecture should help us to understand whether the system being analyzed is healthy or unhealthy.

Moreover, we should also expect there to be a power law distribution of civil societies, with a large number of local civil societies, a moderate number of moderately sized civil societies, and a few very large civil societies. At the largest scale, we could perhaps see a handful of truly overarching civil societies, such as the Anglosphere, which would include such smaller civil societies as the United Kingdom, the United States, Canada, India, Pakistan, Australia, New Zealand, South Africa, and all of the other Anglophone African countries. In addition, there is a Francosphere, of which Canada and Cameroon are also a part (demonstrating how complex things can be, since both include Francophone and Anglophone populations). At the same time, places like India will also have civil societies not readily associated with the Anglosphere. Many former colonies continue to have elements of their civil societies strongly influenced by the cultures, orders, and civil societies of their former colonists, and this creates a number of complexities, as anyone familiar with postcolonial theory knows. A given population is inevitably going to have people embracing the culture of the former colonists, others actively resisting it (meaning they are strongly influenced by it), and others unaffected by either. Further, many African countries in particular were created by unifying some tribes and dividing others—and one should expect to find all three just-mentioned elements in each. Thus, each will constitute its own civil society within the country, and the cooperation and competition among them will constitute the civil society of that particular country as well.

Of course, as anyone familiar with the history of postcolonial Africa knows, many of the nations created by the colonial powers had civil wars, not civil societies. As Sobel et al. observe, "In the literature on international economic development, fractionalization and ethnic diversity have repeatedly been shown to result in inferior economic and social outcomes particularly in African nations" (2010: 270). This is, after all, why Rwanda erupted into civil war. However, cities like New York and Dallas have very high levels of both fractionalization and ethnic diversity. Yet neither one is breaking out in civil war, and both create considerable wealth. Meanwhile, practically homogenous populations like West Virginia are among the poorest populations in the United States. Given that West Virginia and New York State both have the same institutions, more or less, but differ greatly in population diversity, and that New York State has more ethnic diversity than a place like Rwanda, the problem may be the kinds of institutions involved in each kind of civil society. And this, indeed, is what Sobel et al. suggest in their findings: there was a positive correlation between regional cultural diversity and levels of entrepreneurship and wealth creation. They suggest that the weak economies of developing countries come about not from fractionalization, but because these developing countries "most often have weak or failed institutions that do not adequately protect contracts and private property, nor provide a framework of the rule of law" (2010: 282). In contrast, they argue that in countries with good institutions, diversity "helps to promote economic growth and progress" because

> Good formal institutions allow situations in which there are many subgroups with differing informal, cultural, institutions to work together. In the marketplace, mutually-beneficial exchange among people from different cultures helps to make the best use of the local (cultural) knowledge in society, spurring new branches of melded local cultural information, and injecting new combinations into the entrepreneurial process. (2010: 282)

This, of course, would be true not just for the market economy but for the gift, political, and divine economies as well. For example, in the case of the divine economy, the Dialogue Institute of the Southwest (formerly known as the Institute for Interfaith Dialogue) was established by Turkish-American Muslims in Houston, Texas, to create an atmosphere of openness and dialogue among the different religious faiths. Given the diversity, institutions, and culture of Houston, it is perhaps no accident that it was established there—and that it was established by immigrants.

Good institutions are what allow different civil societies, with different cultures, to coexist within larger civil societies. It is therefore vital that we work to create the conditions for the emergence of healthy institutions (which are also kinds of self-organizing processes) that will support the emergence of healthy spontaneous orders, healthy cultures, and healthy civil societies. This means the existence of rule of law, flexible law over rigid legislation, freedom of entry and exit, and freedom of communication. Further, culture can have a very strong impact on the nature of the institutions and spontaneous orders within a given civil society. As Nona Martin and Virgil Storr (2008) observed, culture can create attitudes that can, in turn, create what they call "perverse orders." Of particular note, Martin and Storr observe that homogeneity and the drive toward homogeneity (in racism, classism, and other forms of tribalism) is a fundamental feature of perverse orders. All of this suggests that a healthy culture is vital to the existence of healthy spontaneous orders, which are all necessary for the emergence of healthy civil societies.

Conclusion

Each individual is born a genetically unique individual. Those genes are immediately influenced by the environments in which they find themselves—cellular, in utero, and eventually social. The neural network architectures of our brains are determined by a combination of genes and environment interacting with one another, with our social environments consisting of other people—first those most closely related to us, then more distant relatives, then friends, and inevitably, in the extended order, a large number of strangers with whom we may only ever come into contact but once. Yet, these networks of social individuals contribute to the creation of each of our personalities, helping to individuate each of us more and more. Indeed, the more extensive our networks, the more individuated we become. Thus, the more social we are, the more individuated and the more complex we become. Social complexity drives psychological complexity, which in turn drives social complexity.

This is the reality with which each social scientist must deal. There are benefits to trying to understand the "isolated" psychologies of human beings (although in reality all human psychology is necessarily social psychology), the market, technological, artistic, and other orders, the different cultures, and the different civil societies; however, we must never forget that what we learn in each of the isolated cases must then be reintegrated to create a true understanding of our social structures. Economists can tell us a great deal about how the market works, but many of the details will be culturally informed (Lavoie and Chamlee-Wright), with some cultures working to undermine the market order (Martin and Storr) and others providing a fertile soil for the creation of incredible wealth (McCloskey, 2006). This can range from changes in rhetoric (McCloskey) to the emergence of a culture of reading (Berman 2007).

If we are going to understand different civil societies, and understand their evolution, we are going to have to integrate all of these things—our evolved social psychologies, our cultures, our spontaneous orders, and the various ways in which they can be combined to create civil societies and interacting civil societies of ever-growing complexity (cf. Beck and Cowan, 1996). This means understanding that the economy is not the foundation of all the other orders, but merely one order among many of equal importance to the creation of a civil society. After all, we spend as much or more time engaging in storytelling as in economic transactions—how can one seriously consider the former merely a part of some superstructure built upon economic interactions? And the content of those stories—gossip, novels, television shows, movies, plays, and so on—affect our economic attitudes and, thus, the kinds of laws we support, the kinds of economic interactions in which we are willing (and willing to allow others) to engage and so forth. The same could be said of philosophy, religion—of any of the spontaneous orders discussed above. Note how many of the ways we get stories are via technology, after all. And although few of us will become the Aristotle or Plato of our time, how often do we discuss ethics, what we can or cannot know (epistemology), and so on?—all in the realm of philosophy. And those ideas influence our religious beliefs, economic choices, and so forth. One could go on and on. Indeed, it is the role of every social scientist to do so.

References

Andersson, David Emanuel. 2010. "Cosmos and Taxis in Religious Life: Pattern Regularities and New Challenges." *Studies in Emergent Order*, 3: 172–194, http://studiesinemergentorder.org/past-issues/sieo-volume-3-2010/sieo3-172/.

Beck, Don and Christopher Cowan. 1996. *Spiral Dynamics*. Malden, MA: Blackwell Publishing.

Benedict, Ruth. 1934. Patterns of Culture. Boston, MA: Houghton Mifflin Company.

Berman, Russell A. 2007. *Fiction Sets You Free: Literature, Liberty, and Western Culture*. Iowa City: University of Iowa Press.

Bonner, John T. 1980. *The Evolution of Culture in Animals*. Princeton, NJ: Princeton University Press.

Boulding, Kenneth E. 1985. *The World as a Total System*. Beverly Hills: Sage Publications.

Camplin, Troy. 2010. "The Spontaneous Orders of the Arts." *Studies in Emergent Order*, 3: 195–211, http://studiesinemergentorder.org/past-issues/sieo-volume-3-2010/sieo3-195/.

Collins, Randall. 1998. *The Sociology of Philosophies: A Global Theory of Intellectual Change*. Cambridge, MA: Belknap Press.

Dialogue Institute of the Southwest. 2013. "About Dialogue Institute of the Southwest," http://www.interfaithdialog.org/index.php?option=com_k2&view=item&layout=item&id=296&Itemid=255.

diZerega, Gus. 2013. "Outlining a New Paradigm." *Cosmos + Taxis*. 1(1), http://cosmosandtaxis.files.wordpress.com/2013/11/cosmostaxis_nov18_r1.pdf.

Hayek, F. A. 1973. *Law, Legislation and Liberty: Rules and Order*. Chicago: The University of Chicago Press.

———. 1960. *The Constitution of Liberty*. Chicago: University of Chicago Press.

———. 1948. *Individualism and Economic Order*. Chicago: University of Chicago Press.

Kenrick, Douglas, Jon K. Manner, Jon Butner, Norman P. Li, D. Vaughn Becker, and Mark Schaller. 2002. "Dynamical Evolutionary Psychology: Mapping the Domains of the New Interactionist Paradigm." *Personality and Social Psychology Review*, 6(4): 247–356.

Kenrick, Douglas, Norman P. Li, and Jonathan Butner. 2003. "Dynamical Evolutionary Psychology: Individual Decision Rules and Emergent Social Norms." *Psychological Review*, 110(1): 3–28.

Lavoie, Don and Emily Chamlie-Wright. 2000. *Culture and Enterprise: The Development, Representation and Morality of Business*. New York: Routledge.

Martin, Nona, and Virgil Storr. 2008. "On Perverse Emergent Orders." *Studies in Emergent Order*, 1:73–91.

McCloskey, Deirdre N. 2006. *The Bourgeois Virtues: Ethics for an Age of Commerce*. Chicago, IL: University of Chicago Press.

Mercer, Mike. 2010, August. "Morality in Medieval Economics: A Study on Usury." *The Montreal Review*, http://www.themontrealreview.com/2009/Morality-in-Medieval-Economics.php

Pagel, Mark. 2012. *Wired for Culture: Origins of the Human Social Mind*. New York: W. W. Norton.

Querna, Betsy. 2005. "On the Bookshelf: Finding Our Animal Nature" *U.S. News and World Report*, September 19, 2005, http://www.emory.edu/LIVING_LINKS/OurInnerApe/pdfs/USNews.html.

Saad, Gad. 2011. *The Consuming Instinct*. Amherst, NY: Prometheus Books.

Sabelli, Héctor. 2005. *Bios*. Hackensack, NJ: World Scientific.

Sobel, R. S., N. Dutta, and S. Roy. 2010. "Does Cultural Diversity Increase the Rate of Entrepreneurship?" *The Review of Austrian Economics* 23(3): 269–283

Turner, Frederick. 2005. "Creating a Culture of Gift." *Conversations on Philanthropy II*: 27–58.

Wuthnow, Robert. 1992. "Cultural Change and Sociological Theory." In Hans Haferkamp and Neil J. Smelser (eds.), *Social Change and Modernity*, pp. 257–277. Berkeley: University of California Press.

PART 3

Further Implications for Mind and Society

CHAPTER 5

A Danse Macabre of Wants and Satisfactions: Hayek, Oakeshott, Liberty, and Cognition

Corey Abel and Leslie Marsh

Introduction

In this chapter our aim is to rescue the meaning of liberty from the ministrations of its misguided friends and explore how it relates to human nature, culture, and economic order. Some Austrian economists have embraced liberty as *the* sole value. Despite the overriding "liberty talk" of "soft" libertarians, their position can be assimilated under the liberal-conservative axis, as a species of classical liberalism.[1] Some self-avowed "conservatives" uncritically embrace the market seemingly unaware that its spontaneity and dynamism may well be incompatible with the social values they wish to preserve. However, our primary target is "hard" libertarianism, which, by one prominent theorist's own admission, is thoroughly *il*liberal (Block, 2011). We argue that such a position amounts to a species of absolutism and an extreme case of rationalism, offering at best a vapid account of freedom.

The master argument of this chapter is that *any* liberal position worthy of the name must surely emphasize its skeptical roots and as such be cognizant of the hard-won achievements of free societies. The "hard" libertarian position, by insisting single-mindedly on a narrow interpretation of liberty, leads to a dogmatic and teleocratic (end-governed) conception of political association, and undercuts liberty (Marsh and Hardwick, 2012 and 2013). We explore Oakeshott's arguments on freedom and human action, which avoid the errors of rationalism, and connect these to Hayek's concept of "advanced cognition," and discuss the difference between purposive and nonpurposive political orders. Finally, we explore the importance but also the limitations of freedom understood in terms of economic prosperity and converted into the goal for a society.

Whose Liberalism Is It Anyway?

Historically liberalism comes in several varieties, of which at least three are still highly relevant to considering individual freedom vis-à-vis the state: (a) one holds there is a known objective human good, or a reasonably grounded belief—for example,, John Locke's commendation of "the reasonableness of Christianity"; (b) another says there is an objective human good, but we do not have direct knowledge of it and cannot bring it to fruition except through long-term unplanned progress—for example, John Stuart Mill's "experiments in living"; and (c) another says there is no such thing as an objective good to be known. A person's interests are definable in terms of wants and preferences, desires and inclinations—this variant finds capitalist markets congenial, but can also lend support to utilitarian planning schemes.

Mill observed in *On Liberty* that the major issues of political liberalism had been settled: representative forms of government, a broadening franchise, written constitutions, and other features of most enlightened governments were not much up for debate. The details of such arrangements could be argued, but the major philosophical points seemed to be settled. Mill thought that social liberty was what needed attention, so he described an open society in terms of different styles of living, expressive freedom, and the progressive potential of freedom. At around the same time, liberal society came to be associated with "bourgeois society"—not at all a necessary link, of course—and a ferocious critique began to be mounted, first by Karl Marx, and then by many followers and imitators. Tellingly, Marx and others generally felt the appeal of freedom so strongly that instead of assaulting it directly, they argued that their visions of society actually realized freedom, whereas existing liberal and bourgeois institutions were systematically oppressive and only free in name. Existing social orders were to be overturned not because their stated values were wrong—the way republicans had challenged monarchies for generations—but because they were false representations of those values (Friedman, 1989).

So a curious spectacle has unfolded over the past nearly two hundred years. While nearly all theorists embraced the liberal values of freedom and equality, and while actual regimes around much of the world underwent increasing liberalization, an ongoing debate about the exact meaning of freedom and the exact form of a truly open and free society has run unabated. There are now too many variants of liberalism to count.

Recently, the liberal/communitarian debate and discussion of "positive" and "negative" freedom has kept presses humming; numerous theories of selfhood have emerged; and our "narcissistic society," "bowling alone," and the decline of "social capital," have been lamented. Alongside all this concern for the excesses of freedom and egotism have been efforts to restate and defend liberal principles.

In trying to get a handle on the concept of liberalism, the search for necessary and sufficient conditions is a nonstarter. In other words, there is *no one essential* feature that can be pointed to that "defines" the liberal stance, except, of course, an endorsement of "liberty"—but this core value is variously defined. What makes liberalism distinctively liberal is a specific cluster of *typical* features that, of course, includes: (a) individualism, (b) universalism, (c) egalitarianism, and (d) meliorism (the ability of humans to make progress over natural conditions). Related values may be included, and this is not intended to be an exhaustive list. Samuel Freeman, whom we examine below, for example, belongs to a tradition he calls "high liberal," emphasizing Rawlsian fairness and what he calls "basic liberties." Such basic liberties, for Freeman, include expressive values but not property rights beyond personal possessions. There are some who would balk at calling this liberal at all. Thus, there is a great deal of fluidity within and between ideologies. The different elements are emphasized in some formulations, downplayed in others; some concepts are sidelined, or reinterpreted. This is what Michael Freeden (1994) has termed "ideological morphology." With this in mind we do not think that the Left-Right distinction is very useful since each ideology *cannot* be encased in a set of necessary and sufficient conditions. For example, both conservatism and socialism include an element of communitarianism, and liberalism shares egalitarianism and rationalism with socialism. Thinkers can and do move in and out of ideologies. We should also try to avoid the loaded political uses of these terms. Thus, liberalism should not be associated with the demonized characters of popular discourse, the relativistic and permissive elites. Neither should it be viewed as coextensive with libertarianism or laissez-faire. By the same token, conservatism is not coextensive with laissez-faire. Nor is it synonymous with "rapacious oligarchs," nor again, "true patriots."[2] Speaking of laissez-faire, we think that both libertarians and marketocratic "conservatives" have a muddled sense of liberal individualism. Writing on the confused state of our modern Western political vocabulary, Michael Oakeshott has said, that among the worst of the "current afflictions of liberalism," is the "ignorance of who its true friends are, and the nervy conscience which extends a senile and indiscriminate welcome to everyone who claims to be on the side of progress" (1991: 385). Elsewhere he added, the "saddest of all misunderstandings," is that in which civil association is defended for the sake of prosperity (1991: 457; and see 1975: 241–242) (cf. Nell, chapter 6, this volume).

Of course, individualism is yet another deeply contested term. In the liberal tradition (Rawls, Hayek, Mill, Smith, Kant, Bentham, Constant, Tocqueville, Green, Bosanquet, Croce, and many more besides), what this amounts to is a cluster of related and overlapping ideas: (a) individuals are the ultimate units of moral value; (b) there is no social good over and above individuals; (c) individual well-being requires people to make their own choices as far as possible; (d) the moral unity of the human species is affirmed and historical circumstances have secondary importance (universalism); (e) all men have the same moral status (this *moral* egalitarianism has been transmuted into a purely materialist egalitarianism characteristic of social or distributive justice theorists).

Today's conservatives, as pointed out above, are not "counterrevolutionaries," so much as reluctant liberals, critics of the excess and ideological zeal of the more radical wings of liberalism. In fact they embrace most if not all the features of liberalism.[3] Where conservatives are distinct is (a) in being (mostly) hesitant to embrace universalism, preferring a more historically grounded communitarianism; (b) rejecting the Cartesian and rationalistic conception of the individual; (c) being less hopeful and more skeptical about the prospects of large-scale social transformation; and, (d) in various quarters, embracing varying degrees of "social" or "values" orientations opposed to some aspect of modernity. Hayek has encapsulated these traits in his comment that "Unlike liberalism, with its fundamental belief in the long-range power of ideas, conservatism is bound by the stock of ideas inherited at a given time. And since it does not really believe in the power of argument, its last resort is generally a claim to superior wisdom, based on some self-arrogated superior quality" (Hayek, 1960: 404). And further, "Though the liberal certainly does not regard all change as progress, he does regard the advance of knowledge as one of the chief aims of human effort and expects from it the gradual solution of such problems and difficulties as we can hope to solve" (Hayek, 1960: 404).

Michael Oakeshott is most often called a conservative, but has proven to be hard to classify, with some writers calling him liberal, others republican, and still others a critic of liberalism (see Franco, 1990; Coats, 1985 and 1992; Sandel, 1984). From our perspective, he is the most profound articulator and defender of human freedom in the twentieth century, and he sheds interesting light on these Hayekian observations. It is not that a conservative must reject argument, tout court. Oakeshott, for example, rejects a specific malformation of reason as applied to politics, which he calls rationalism. His antirationalist arguments are in defense of an Aristotelian practical reason appropriate to political affairs (Abel, 2005: 37–60; Callahan, 2013: 50–52; Swanson, 2013: 21–38). And while he is skeptical of progress, he does not deny it so much as point out the dangers of adopting a specific substantive end to be pursued by the exercise of government power. Such "teleocratic" progressivism carries a specific political danger, to wit: it justifies ever-increasing power and discretionary administration, undercutting free association and rule of law.[4]

Instead of claiming that conservatives are antirational, we note that for conservatives *tradition is rational*. Where a tradition is the only reliable resource, its disregard is irrational. Practical reasoning interrogates and applies a tradition. For the conservative, one is always dealing with a reflective tradition, not an inert pattern of habitual behavior (Marsh, 2010: 248–267). We will explore below how embedded individualism is consistent with dynamic traditions, but a conservative position is, by virtue of its conserving, always oriented to something more than individual choices as such. The communitarian element in conservatism does not, however, make communitarianism as such a conservative perspective. Conservatism distinctively combines communitarianism with the complexity thesis and limited government.

The whole of Oakeshott's essay "On Being Conservative" is animated by the effort to defend conservatism (or the conservative disposition with *respect to politics*)[5]: (a) without recourse to large-scale religious or metaphysical beliefs and (b) without endorsing a more general traditionalism or communitarianism. It is a wholly modern appreciation of how we live now, what we have become. Radical individualists such as David Hume, Michel de Montaigne, Blaise Pascal, and Thomas Hobbes—skeptics all, it should be noted—are good guides in this regard. "It is not at all inconsistent," Oakeshott wrote, "to be conservative in respect of government and radical in respect of almost every other activity" (1991: 435).[6] In other words, there is only a contingent connection between a disposition against change in one's personal life and circumstances, and a conservative disposition in politics. All of life involves the resolution of incoherencies and thus a commitment to change. The conservative's political restraint has to do with appreciating the complexity and dynamism of social orders, and understanding the human stake in altering those orders, which involve the use of compulsion and all the attendant temptations to abuse.

As Hayek lays it out, there are indeed very few true conservatives in today's world; those who believe in using the state's power to reorder social life betray a kinship with socialists to whom they are usually opposed. Also, many conservatives employ a rationalistic and ideological political style (often distinctly fundamentalist in flavor) and vocabulary, being in fact "traditionalist" rather than traditional. But it remains true that most who call themselves conservative are in fact classical liberals. According to Hayek's scheme, Oakeshott would be characterized as a classical liberal.

> What in Europe was called "liberalism" was [in America] the common tradition on which the American polity had been built: thus the defender of the American tradition was a liberal in the European sense. (Hayek, 1960: 400)

This point echoes Alexis de Tocqueville's interpretation of America as democratic from the start. But it is largely true outside the United States as well, in Oakeshott's Britain, for example, as classical liberalism has roots going back beyond Hobbes to the late medieval period. So to defend classical liberalism is in fact to defend tradition. Of course, Europe has other traditions, but these have largely receded, with surviving monarchs being mainly ceremonial heads of state. Hayek errs by identifying conservatives with resistance to change and a lack of ideas, and liberals with the "power of ideas"—which makes liberals somewhat antitraditional and rationalistic. This is not his whole position, of course. Another point he makes is that

> conservatives are inclined to use the powers of government to prevent change or to limit its rate to whatever appeals to the more timid mind. In looking forward, they lack the faith in the spontaneous forces of adjustment which makes the liberal accept changes without apprehension, even though he does not know how the necessary adaptations will be brought about. (Hayek, 1960: 400)

There is no timidity in Oakeshott's conservatism; the reasons he gives for being conservative in respect to governance have solely to do with limiting power and enjoying reliable legal norms. Like Hayek, he grasps situated rationality and attendant social complexity.

Oakeshott has no interest in defending established hierarchies. He would agree with the liberal Hayek that economic concentrations of power are among the powers that must be limited. (Carson, 2014, applies a Hayekian critique of central planning to the dynamics of large corporations.)

In what sense might moderate libertarianism be considered a species of liberalism? While we are not out of sympathy with several aspects of moderate or "soft" libertarianism, we are of the view that many of these concerns can be assimilated within existing liberal-conservative political traditions, which therefore renders this variant of libertarianism not particularly distinctive.

An Illiberal High Liberal and An Illiberal Libertarian

An exchange between Freeman and Walter Block is instructive, in showing how the progressive Left and the "hard" libertarian Right both veer away from liberalism properly understood. Freeman has written,

> Liberalism holds that there are certain individual liberties that are of fundamental political significance. These liberties are fundamental or basic in that they are preconditions on the pursuit of other social values, such as achieving economic efficiency, promoting the general welfare, and moderating the degree of inequality in the distribution of income and wealth." (2011: 19)

Freeman is not always careful to observe the distinction he makes between "classical" (seventeenth- to nineteenth-century political) and "high" (Rawlsian) liberalism, but it is a worthwhile distinction, so we will stress it. The liberalism Freeman is here "defining" is obviously the "high" kind. With alacrity he makes "basic freedoms" expressly and unambiguously instrumental to other aims. This is hardly a defense of freedom. Classical liberals have long recognized that even basic, enumerated, and, in some nations, constitutionally guaranteed liberties are not so absolute as to allow the disintegration of society, the commission of gross injustice, or the making of all governance impossible. Nonetheless, classical liberals would accept certain limitations on freedom only because of necessity, not in service of some desirable aim. This is because there is no aim beyond freedom itself. Living freely is its own reward, and there is no larger goal to be served by it.

In another essay, Freeman says liberalism holds that

> there is a plurality of intrinsic goods . . . [and] different ways of living worth affirming for their own sake; . . . having the freedom to determine and pursue their *conceptions* of the good is essential to [individuals'] living a good life, . . . [and] necessary to individuals' good is that their freely adopted conceptions of the good be consistent with justice. (2002: 105)

The first two conditions sound classically liberal. The last condition, however, veers off into a position subversive of liberty. It is one thing to say that license is not liberty, or to join Immanuel Kant in saying that true freedom is found in morally autonomous agency. It is another matter to say individuals' life plans—supposedly worth affirming for their own sakes—must conform to "justice." This is especially true since Freeman thinks of justice in strictly Rawlsian terms, as the redistribution of income and wealth for the sake of achieving a high degree of social equality. There are few people in modern societies whose life plans really embrace the Rawlsian ideal; they are mostly concentrated in academic departments of political science.

Freeman's comments come from an essay that attacks libertarianism and calls it "illiberal." Our view is that most libertarianism falls squarely within classical liberalism. However, Block takes the charge and defends his "illiberal" position. In responding to Freeman's argument that libertarianism merely turns on a contractual sense of ownership and leads to a form of feudalism, Block happily denies that he is a liberal. He is denying that he is a Rawlsian "high" liberal, but he goes even further, expressly pointing out that his "hard" libertarian stance excludes traditional liberal arguments about necessary restraints on freedom. In fact, he goes so far as to justify slavery contracts, provided they are "voluntary." In that regard, he is neither a "high" nor a "classical" liberal. His view is in fact *illiberal* and that is his badge of honor. Below, we will examine some of Freeman's and Block's claims in detail to show how both of them suffer from a tendency toward rationalistic expressions of abstract ideals, and endorse teleocratic conceptions of the state. Even Block, in his near anarchism, ends up a teleocrat.

Freeman objects to Block's slavery argument on grounds that there is no exit, which is a good point. And, he points out that a slavery contract, if it is enforceable by courts, has broader implications beyond the contracting parties, becoming part of the legal structure of society, and not merely a private agreement. This is a good point insofar as it shows how a free society is a more complex web of relationships than merely contracting individuals. However, the point, and especially Freeman's phrasing of it as requiring others "to participate in [the slave's] civic and moral debasement" (Freeman, 2002: 111–112), opens the door to teleocratic excess. For, if we apply this standard, we might find many social arrangements that are "debasing" by someone's standards (e.g., any court's judgment that upheld the right of one over another who could plausibly be characterized as a "victim" regardless of the narrow meaning of the law as applied to the case). Then the role of the courts becomes the imposition of positive duties. So in rejecting slave contracts, Freeman replaces them with a powerfully teleocratic and paternalistic vision of state power.

Like Midas, he does this in everything he touches: "Society has a duty to support an education system to even out class barriers" (2002: 116), he says, giving a teleological rationale for education, which might be more straightforwardly defended as a simple public good. He denies that a "high liberal" regime would attack inequality in such a way as to "radically alter or abolish the family" (2002: 117) yet he gives no reason why, nor does he note that some liberals like Martha Nussbaum have made exactly this claim. He claims explicitly that property beyond basic personal possessions is not a basic right (2002: 114), and further, that "Without sufficient income and wealth one's liberties and opportunities are worth little" (2002: 117), thereby expressly denigrating liberty as a core value. He displays a rationalistic and teleocratic character in saying that "property rights should be decided by asking which system of property laws best enables citizens to realize their freedom" (2002: 119)—as if the possession of rights is not itself a manifestation of freedom, and further, as if rights exist in some noetic realm where we can simply choose among different systems, giving little or no regard to the historically achieved rights embedded throughout our legal system. Such embedded rights are just detritus to be swept away as the high liberal pursues his Rawlsian vision.

Freeman is stronger when criticizing the excesses of libertarianism, although not all his points stick. For example, the argument that libertarian doctrines of ownership imply feudalism is strange (2002: 147–148), and Freeman does not even acknowledge the ways in which a planned and centrally controlled economy teleologically managed for the pursuit of "social justice" can become a system of privilege and preference that resembles feudalism.[7] He goes quite haywire in asserting that the real point of libertarian arguments is simply to minimize political duties, "in particular any enforceable obligations to transfer market-acquired holdings to benefit the disadvantaged" (2002: 126, and cf. 2002: 150). In projecting the motives of his enemy to be the narrowly ideological aim of reducing transfer payments, Freeman underestimates his opponent's radicalism, and reveals his own teleological view of government. He indicates that his own view is to use state power to enforce such transfers, for a specific end.

Freeman does strike a blow against Block's slavery argument by pointing out that the slave's will loses its capacity to change. As noted above, he had tried to distance himself from the classical liberal critique of slavery, but later comes close to recapitulating it, pointing out that in the case of an enforcement action under a slave contract, the voluntariness of the contract is in doubt: "The fact that earlier she committed herself to act as she now is forced to act does not negate the fact that she is now being forced to act against her will" (2002: 132 n56).[8] He does successfully show the absurdity of libertarian rationalism, although without phrasing it in these terms. The problem of contractual enforceability arises out of the libertarian desire for a kind of geometric consistency in claiming that contracts are enforceable because they express the will. But if this is so, then all contracts would have to be valid, yet libertarians wish to prohibit contracts for murder and other "criminal" activities. The point is that a simple principle like "respect for will" is not a sufficient basis to have a workable legal and practical method of determining which contracts are or are not enforceable. Freeman has displayed his own rationalism, but at least he sees Block's rationalism.

Block, in language shockingly like Freeman's, also wishes to end all political debates once and for all by providing "one, single, solitary answer," (2011: 538) to the problem of the use of force, grounded on libertarian principles of voluntariness as the basis of social order. But this adherence to abstract principle makes him strangely unable to differentiate cases of the boxer, the prisoner, and the slave. All of them, he says, are where they are by virtue of their own past choices (2011: 550). But this is the merest tautology. The boxer is not, as Block suggests "in some sense debased" and "in distress"—he has voluntarily taken up a rule-bound and structured sport, trained for it and decided to do it, for intrinsic and/or extrinsic reasons of his own. The prisoner, on the other hand, is not at all a willing participant—notwithstanding some fancy Hegelian moves to reconcile the immediate and subjective will with some higher and objective will. In a simple practical sense, the prisoner does to want to be imprisoned. And it is not clear why, short of abusive treatment or errant prosecution, imprisonment is debasing. It is the straightforward result of violating laws and being convicted. The "voluntary slave," however, is an entirely different case, since she supposedly relinquishes all freedom forever, not as a form of play, nor temporarily, nor as an instance of legally sanctioned punishment for specific offense, but permanently, as a personal choice. In boxing, the physical blows undergone are not "punishment" at all (in spite of sportscasters' oft-used metaphor: "a punishing blow!").; in the second case, Block should recognize it as legitimate retaliatory violence, or punishment; and in the third case of the slave, the issue is relinquishment of will, regardless of actual treatment.

Block's inability to draw simple distinctions is a sure sign of either sophistical intent or a complete substitution of dogmatic adherence to abstract principles for practical and prudent reasoning. As Callahan said about Block, "one suspects that the more outlandish the conclusion, the happier Block is at reaching it" (2013: 57, and cf. diZerega, 2014). Callahan has argued, with numerous examples drawn from Hoppe, Block,

Rothbard, and others in what we are calling the "hard" libertarian camp, that examples of rationalistic abstraction and extremism abound, from Hoppe's teleological claim that a libertarian society would have to exclude dissent, to Rothbard's endorsement of police coercion and more (2013: 48–67).

Rather than dilate further upon the absurdities of "hard" libertarian rationalism or the teleological assumptions of "high" liberalism, we would like to note that operating under both of them, competing conceptions are flawed conceptions of agency and social relations. On the "hard libertarian" side, there is raw voluntariness elevated to the sole moral and legal standard. But this works neither as a description of agency, nor of free action, nor of social relations built on freedom. On the "high liberal" side, there is at least the recognition that agency is embedded within practices and institutions, that society is more than a concatenation of individual contracts. However, this insight is obscured by the hasty desire to insist upon redistribution for the sake of equality, undermining freedom by imposing a rigid vision of "political duty" on all.

Thus, what is needed is a reformulated classical liberalism resting, first, upon embedded individualism, not on atomic or hedonic egotism, and second, on a combination of epistemic and moral humility.

SITUATED INDIVIDUALISM

Our account owes debts to Oakeshott and Hayek. We find them, in spite of some differences of emphasis, to be largely in agreement on key points relating to both individuality and the reasons for endorsing a limited view of government. Both Hayek and Oakeshott jointly and severally reject any notion of the state in which the members are related in terms of a common, substantive purpose, whether it be religious salvation, moral virtue, or economic productivity or redistribution. As we will see below, Oakeshott deploys a distinction between purposive and nonpurposive association that has resonances with Hayek's well-known distinction between instrumental and spontaneous orders.

We argue that (a) the commitment to abstract individualism undermines the Austrian insight that posits *situated* agents and (b) the notion of individualism is not coextensive with individuality, unlike hard libertarians who seem committed to a form of abstract individualism manifest as social atomism.

Asocial theorizing is the stock-in-trade to a whole range of philosophical endeavor. Identity in the canonical Lockean tradition, epistemology in the Platonic-Cartesian tradition, and orthodox philosophy of mind are asocial. This asocial methodological tendency is found in neuroscience as it is in the neoclassical tradition of economics. By contrast, social identity and social epistemology in the (Marxist) sociological tradition, in stressing ubiquitous sociality, has tended to posit inflated social ontologies. With these two extreme poles, never the twain shall meet. But things have been changing. Communitarianism, a social theory that reached its zenith in 1980s, is in large measure a critique of asociality. The individualistic epistemology characteristic of the Platonic-Cartesian tradition has belatedly been engaging the social dimensions to knowledge by taking account, for example, of the ways cognition is culturally saturated and distributed across virtual and physical networks. So-called "Austrian" economics has long since been challenging the rationality of the fictional *homo economicus* so characteristic of neoclassical economics and of central planning-type rationalism. Libertarianism has also been devoted to a stark individualism that at times defends freedom by an embrace of an asocial view of human nature.

Individualism has many, often overlapping as well as some incongruent connotations. In moral and political philosophy, individual persons are the ultimate units of moral worth. Individualism in the philosophy of social science hinges on the extent to which individuals' cognitive states are held to be causally dependent upon their social milieu. Furthermore, could all statements about political and other institutions be reduced to statements referring purely to individuals and their interactions? Methodological individualism is the view that this is possible; social holism denies this (Marsh and Hardwick, 2012).

The terms "individualism" and "individuality" are, like most of our political vocabulary, ambiguous. Tocqueville, a great supporter of individuality, nonetheless wrote an excoriating critique of "individualism"—which would be better called egotism, or egocentrism, as his analysis makes clear. But as a result of conflating or confusing these terms, or associating the concept of individuality with egocentrism, powerfully anti-individualist forces have made headway, such that many conservatives and even classical liberals are hesitant to defend individuality. We would like to suggest that in general, "individualism" is best confined to a methodological use, while "individuality" is adjectival and refers to the emergent qualities of situated agency (diZerega and Denis, both in this volume, explore individualism and methodological individualism in depth).

Another problem is that several doctrines of human nature have been interwoven with the liberal tradition as it emerged historically Thus it is widely believed that to agree with Hobbes about the need for stable political authority and the covenantal basis of legitimate authority, one has to view humans as essentially selfish.[9] Jean-Jacques Rousseau and the Scottish moral sense philosophers tried to correct what they saw as a deficiency in Hobbes, and further compounded the belief that freedom was somehow tied up with a particular doctrine of human nature. Man can be free because he is not selfish, but sympathetic. The history of economics is littered with attempts to found economic activity on theories of human motivation or human nature: rational actors, utility maximizers, and hedonists have naturally seemed to fit with the view of economic activity as profit seeking. But it is not necessary to endorse a general theory of human selfishness to point out that people respond to incentives. (See below, Oakeshott's account of agency; see also Denis and Nell, both in this volume.)

These old debates about the relation of free agency to social order have hardly abated. Over the past 30 years, debate has raged in political theory between "communitarians" and "liberals." Much of this debate has revolved around the claim that liberals (conflating both classical liberals and high liberals like Freeman) assume an egoistic conception of the self, while communitarians argue for a "dialogic," "embedded," "social," or "contextual" self. But as with Marxist overstatements of social ontology, some communitarians have gone so far as to regret modern individuality itself, and raised the standard of an anti-individualist "community." Whatever justice there maybe in the communitarian charges against liberals, the communitarians too often fail to see that a situated self is compatible with a robust individuality. The self is neither exclusively private nor public, but partakes of both.

It may be no accident that an entirely asocial conception of selfhood has emerged historically alongside scientific rationalism and the consumer society. A link is suggested by the great novelist, philosopher, and critic Walker Percy, who wrote,

> The common mark of the theorist and the consumer is that neither knows who he is or what he wants outside of theorizing and consuming.
>
> This is so because the theorist is not encompassed by his theory. One's self is always a leftover from one's theory.
>
> For even if one becomes passionately convinced of Freudian theory or Marxist theory at three o'clock of a Wednesday afternoon, what does one do with oneself at four o'clock?
>
> The consumer, who thought he knew what he wanted—the consumption of goods and services of scientific theory—is not in fact satisfied, even when the services offered are such techniques as "personal growth," "emotional maturity," "consciousness-raising," and suchlike.
>
> The face of the denizen of the present age who has come to the end of theory and consumption and "personal growth" is the face of sadness and anxiety. (1991: 311)

The core argument on offer is that whatever else sociality may be, by definition it cannot reside solely within an individual. An individual, whatever else it may be, exists in relationships with other individuals, embedded within various practices, foremost native and acquired languages. (See also Camplin and diZerega, both in this volume). As a result, we resist attempts to define the person in narrow terms such as an "ego" severed from tradition or context. The same mentality that analytically breaks down the experienced world into "clear and distinct" ideas also separates the human self into a series of discrete mental processes and external relationships. While this method has undoubted power in many spheres, it has also proved misleading in understanding humans as they live in society. One sophisticated attempt to define a very different notion of situated agency is from Charles Taylor, who argues that the conception of the good life, indeed our very own character and identity—are inextricably linked and constituted by self-interpretations (1984 and 1989; see also Percy, 1991: 312).

Community is, then, a structural precondition of human agency, including, of course, moral agency. Taylor shows how this strong position can stay clear of the excessive social ontologies of Marxists and others, and retain an appreciation of individuality. Even an individualist political tradition such as liberalism, which places great emphasis on the dignity and freedom of each person, must also commit itself to certain communal values. At a minimum, an individualist social ethic must be committed to maintaining those communal structures and institutions that themselves permit an individualist ethic to flourish.

Communitarians argue that the liberal emphasis on schemes of rights is problematic because it reduces persons to self-interested, rights-bearing atoms who demand only negative freedom in order to pursue individualistic goals. Pursuit of the good, they argue, is not a radically individualistic endeavor, but is only meaningful in the context of a community with historically developed ethical traditions. It is because we are socialized into these inherited ethical traditions that we can begin to formulate our conception of the good. Persons are not metaphysical, "unencumbered selves" who can stand back from all of their inherited values and communal attachments and "freely" choose their ends, as liberals suppose.[10] But in attacking a totally unencumbered self, they are attacking a straw man, albeit one midwifed in Cambridge, Massachusetts. A fully situated and robustly individualistic account of agency is available from Oakeshott, to whom we now turn.

Oakeshott's account of the self is developed alongside his critique of rationalism, and further developed in his account of human conduct. In the provocatively titled "Rational Conduct," Oakeshott criticizes the epistemological underpinnings of rationalism and attacks the view that the mind is "an independent instrument capable of dealing with experience"

(1991: 106). Beliefs, ideas, and knowledge are mind, for Oakeshott, not something the mind acquires. If the acquired contents of the mind themselves compose the mind, then a human being's consciousness is formed through experience. (As diZerega, 2014, points out "real people are not abstractions."). This view is not deterministic, since the consciousness of an agent also questions, doubts and responds to the world. *This mindful responsiveness is freedom.* Oakeshott's idea of freedom avoids subjectivism and determinism because mindful human activity is always manifested in (not bounded by) concrete, specific activities, or "practices." Oakeshott's view that action occurs within practices stands in contrast to the rationalist's view that a purpose and means to realize that purpose are premeditatively determined, independently of considerations of habit, custom, or tradition (1991: 106).

Participation in concrete practices means for Oakeshott that even a person's desires emerge in the context of distinct activities, not from axiomatic principles or given preferences (see also Nell, this volume).

> [T]o say that (a man) has a desire for something is only another way of saying that he is being active in a certain manner—e.g. the manner of activity involved in reaching out his hand to turn off the hot water, in making a request . . . in looking up the times of the trains to Scotland, in contemplating with pleasure a meeting with a friend. These activities are not activities which . . . exhibit or give evidence of an antecedent state of desire; they are themselves the characteristic activities of desiring. (1991: 124–125)

This can be contrasted with Rothbard's "demonstrated preferences," in which action merely *demonstrates* given preferences. Bare desire has no shape, while ideas isolated from conduct are barren. Desiring and reasoning are both part of the flow of experience. What we desire reflects our learning, and our learning is the education of desire. Self and practice are intertwined. An agent is free in the same way a speaker of a language is free; the constraint of practices merely gives structure and meaning without determining the utterance. (Cf. Holcombe, 2014, who points to language as an example of spontaneous order.)

Oakeshott first laid out these ideas in the 1930s and 1940s, but similar currents have been moving in several areas of philosophy, and are seen in Hayek's theory of situated cognition.

One major contemporary school that has developed insights similar to Oakeshott's is enactivism, a species of situated cognition having a threefold overlapping character: enactive, embedded, and extended. It is *enactive* in that mind does not merely respond to a given world; mind is enacted through a particularized history of environmental coupling: perception is an act of interpretation and the generation of meaning. It is *embedded* in that mind necessarily offloads and harvests knowledge through practices and traditions, artifacts that afford epistemic efficiencies. It is *extended* in that whatever practices and traditions may be, they cannot reside solely within an individual: continuity can only be mediated, albeit imperfectly, through a web of social artifacts that contains its own immanent standard of epistemic weight regarding its methodological, conceptual, and empirical problems.

For Oakeshott and Hayek, this is the mark of advanced cognition—humankind's ability to diffuse propositional and practical knowledge through external epistemic structures. For Oakeshott, this knowledge is "suspended" in traditions and practices; for Hayek, knowledge exists within a "network" as spontaneous or complex adaptive orders. (Camplin's account of culture has resonances here, in this volume.)

Some have said that knowing-how is the "very essence of creative cognition" (Hutto, 2005: 389–405). For Oakeshott and Hayek, traditions are inherently complex, because they are generated by infinitely fine-grained, constantly shifting, local, and ephemeral variables (Marsh, 2010). Practical knowledge (or know-how) cannot be reduced, abridged, or restated propositionally (knowledge-that) without remainder. For Hayek, that implies a twofold constraint: (a) no single mind can apprehend all the knowledge required to order an entire society by planning, because of the necessary dispersion of knowledge and (b) no single mind can deal with the complexity or amount of detail that would be required to guide even the simplest actions if certainty is our criterion of rightness or predictable result. Andy Clark calls this the "spreading of epistemic credit" (1997: 69).[11] Situated agents are perpetually responding to and redefining their environment without having recourse to an explicit range of alternatives. Instead, the virtuosity of their imagination gives order and depth to their analysis of their situation. For both Oakeshott and Hayek, Gilbert Ryle's celebrated critique of the Cartesian project provided a useful conceptual underpinning to their own critiques of the rationalist propensity to view thought as strictly propositional (Marsh, 2012 and 2013).

In order to stress that embedded agency is nondeterministic and worlds apart from any doctrine of egoism or hedonism, Oakeshott's account of conduct is helpful. In *On Human Conduct*, Oakeshott emphasizes the thoughtful character of human experience by distinguishing intelligent from nonintelligent activities. Human conduct is always intelligent—even when it is not markedly bright. "An agent is one who is recognized to have an understanding of himself in terms of his wants and powers and an understanding of the components of the world he inhabits; and action is recognized as illustrative of that understanding" (1975: 32).

The placement of human conduct in the realm of "intelligent goings-on" means that the view of man as under the sway of biological, psychological or other nonintelligent drives is modally irrelevant. As Oakeshott points out, a congenitally deaf man, while perhaps not the most likely promoter of noise abatement, is not excluded from

> understanding his own situation in terms of "noise," e.g.: "I am the deaf husband of a wife who suffers greatly from the noise of air-traffic." Indeed, the most devoted promoter of "noise abatement" may be one who, by circumstances never himself suffers the evil he wishes to reduce. (1975, 37–38)

As Taylor called humans "self-interpreting animals," Oakeshott insists on "self-understanding" as the constitutive basis of agency. In recognizing the situation as his own, the agent is involved in a judgment about the world that is not confined to his subjective point of view.[12]

An agent's immersion in the world does not rob him of his individuality. What would deny individuality according to Oakeshott is an assertion that all conduct traces back to some primordial impulse. An embedded agency has no place for assumptions of selfishness.

Oakeshott adds that what is true of the agent's diagnosis is true also of his action. "His act is ineluctably his own, and its outcome will unavoidably be himself in a new situation, but it does not follow that what he intends, the meaning of his action, must be a self-gratification" (1975: 53). As Austrians are well aware, to act is to choose, and where there is choice, there is the possibility of acting on another's behalf. And this possibility exists, not because of a faculty of will operating independently of biological laws or other urges, but in virtue of the agent's character as a reflective consciousness. "Agents are related to one another in terms of understandings . . . they may care for one another because they can think of one another. The myth of the necessarily egocentric agent is a denial of agency" (1975: 53). He might have added to this: so too, the myth of the necessarily sympathetic man. (Cf. Denis chapter 1 and Nell chapter 3, both in this volume.)

To the extent most modern political theories and economics take account of motive, they tend to reduce all motive to a single natural cause—humans are selfish, or utility maximizing, or sympathetic.[13] Such views deny agency. They also end up giving a very constrained view of human conduct. Combined with the tendency to characterize all social practices as "markets," it is not hard to reach a view of humans as materialistic strivers, and a free society as one based solely on unbridled exploitation of the earth's resources—exactly as critics of liberty are wont to do, from neo-Marxists down to communitarian sociologists.[14]

Individuality is the disposition to enjoy the freedom inherent in agency, and to make a virtue out of self-determination. This is far from mere crass self-interestedness.

A further important point about agency and selfhood as understood by Oakeshott is rooted in his idea of modality. He uses the idea of modality to differentiate different fields of activity and knowledge, but also to differentiate the sort of character that corresponds to the activity. A scientist, for example, is an abstract *persona* (further specifiable as a "medical physicist"), not to be confused with the natural individual human being who is a scientist, but who may also be husband, son, father, business partner, and poet. *Civis*, or citizen, is the *persona* of agents legally related to one another in civil association. However, this civil identity does not exhaust an agent's identity, or deny the possibility of other idiomatic identities.

> Thus, two persons may be joined, as husband and wife, in a legal mode of relationship, civil or ecclesiastical, but they may also be related in the categorically different terms of love, affection, friendship, and so on, and further they may be partners in a business enterprise. And while a teacher and his pupil may have a legal and a commercial relationship, they have also an educational relationship whose terms are neither those of law nor of commerce. . . . the subject in a mode of relationship is always an abstraction, a *persona*, a person in respect of being related to others in terms of distinct and exclusive conditions. (1983: 119–120)

It is characteristic of Oakeshott's efforts to differentiate activities and inquiries, and to honor boundaries of relevance, that he does not begin his political theory with a conception of "the self" simply, or "human nature." In addition to being *embedded*, the Oakeshottian self is modally *differentiated*. Such differentiated selfhood is far more sophisticated than what is on offer from most political theorists, economists, and others. In Rawls, for example, and in rational choice, and in all the critics of liberalism, there is a persistent but unspoken assumption that human beings have not only a generic nature but also a singular one. The 'self' that is assumed in debates in political theory is discussed as if we operated behind a "veil of ignorance" in dealing with our parents, our priest, and our policeman alike, or that we are utility maximizers, even when we lose ourselves in passionate love or sacrifice all that is necessary to rear children. Too often, accounts of agency and individuality are reductionist, turning even lovers and poets into selfish genetic machines, baskets of neuroses, or bundles of abstract desires. Oakeshott's response to this narrowness is to say that the *civis* is a narrowly defined aspect of the whole self. Thus, his account of the subject of civil association excludes, but does not deny, much that we ordinarily recognize as taking place within the state or within the lives of individuals.[15]

MODES OF POLITICAL ASSOCIATION

Unlike cognitive scientists, philosophers, and economists, many of whom shared insights with Oakeshott, his views of agency and conduct directly connect to his political theory. Oakeshott offers a compelling variant of classical liberalism and the rule of law. The most interesting aspect of his theory is its distinguishing two modes of association. While Hayek's critique of state planning is justly famous, his efforts to sketch a "constitution of liberty" tend to an ahistorical and abstract formulation that is somewhat in tension with his embedded view of cognition. Oakeshott, on the other hand, presents his two "ideal types" (the "modes of association") as being derived from the historical experience of modern European states. The two modes are telic and nontelic, or instrumental and moral. Oakeshott is at pains to stress that actual states have always blended and mixed the tendencies, but it still helps to distinguish them for theoretical clarity.

Oakeshott's conception of civil association as moral association means both that it is a noninstrumental or formal relationship and that it possesses a distinctive moral character given by the historically achieved disposition of a collection of people living together. Oakeshott's view of law as *formal* does not mean that law is entirely neutral with respect to moral concerns. Law embodies at the same time as it narrows or focuses those concerns. However, to acknowledge that law reflects a community's moral traditions (*Sittlichkeit*) is worlds away from envisioning the government as a moral educator and leader of social reform. Civil association in no way involves a moralizing state's acting to bring about "the good." For the state to define the happiness of its members by choosing specific substantive satisfactions to pursue would be for it to override the agent's freedom to determine conduct on the basis of his or her own beliefs or understandings. If civil association leaves agents free to determine their own satisfactions, can freedom be described as the aim of civil association? This is a tempting and common formulation, but freedom is a formal quality of conduct, a condition enjoyed, but not a substantive condition of things to be attained. Freedom, like security, characterizes civil association, but is not an end or consequence; rather, these are "inherent in its character" (1983: 161; see also, 1975: 157–158).

Fostering individuality might also be thought of as the aim of civil association. This historic disposition, however, is more like a language that facilitates speech without determining utterance. In addition, the very notion of individuality means that the substantive actions that define the pursuit of happiness are chosen by the individual, and hence cannot be specified by a general norm of individualism, nor made the object of a common pursuit.

A robust individualism is perfectly consistent with community or sociality, and in no way implies isolation, anomie, egoism, and the rest. (Camplin, this volume, makes a similar point.) Participation in voluntary associations does not compromise individuality for the same reason it does not compromise freedom—because participation or nonparticipation is a choice of the individual, and he is free to quit if he no longer holds the purposes pursued to be worthy. The state, however, is a compulsory, not a voluntary, organization. Thus, this freedom to dissociate oneself from the pursuit of projects does not exist.[16]

A civil association can be compulsory yet maintain freedom, because it is merely an association in terms of laws, and not in terms of a goal or purpose. (Nell, 2014, focuses on the political process rather than the mode of association.) This formal notion of law leaves individuals free in the sense that their assent to it does not require assent to the merits of some political project, and in the sense that their actions are self-chosen responses to contingent situations in which the legally specified conditions of conduct are taken into account "adverbially," but do not determine the outcome.

A state organized as an association to pursue a common end compels its members to participate in some overall project. This denies freedom, by breaking the link between belief and conduct. An individual is obliged to assist in the pursuit of an end he does not hold to be worthy.[17] In a compulsory association, the relationship of agents is in terms of authority, but authority, like associations, appears in two modes. In the enterprise association, the telos defines the association. Its rules, or laws, are authoritative to the extent that they serve the achievement of the end. In a civil association, the rules' authority rests in the associates' assent, which is grounded only in the recognition of a rule's place in a system of interconnected rules. Thus, the difference between instrumental rules (those of an enterprise association) and noninstrumental rules (those of a civil association) may be described as different ways by which a legal rule can possess authority.[18]

Skeptical Liberalism

As Hayek affirms in "Why I Am Not a Conservative," the classical liberal view is a skeptical one. Oakeshott is even more of a skeptic than Hayek, who holds on to a residual Enlightenment faith in progress and science. For Oakeshott in particular, the differentiation of experience brought by his modal epistemology results in a strange but profound skepticism.

Oakeshott is not a Pyrrhic skeptic who refutes and denies knowledge. Instead he is everywhere defending the integrity and independence of modes of experience, of association, and of selfhood. His skepticism is founded on (a) the insufficiency of any mode to conceptually and propositionally encompass the whole gamut of human experience and (b) the inability of any mode to resolve the problems or settle the arguments of another. The historian may tell the history of science, but in doing so he in no way answers a scientific question or contributes to science. Modality might be called the epistemology of humility or the metaphysics of modesty. Thus, Oakeshott is no irrationalist, but holds a deeply skeptical worldview that undergirds his antirationalism and antiperfectionism. He goes deeper in his skepticism than Hayek. Since Hayek has defined the liberal position as skeptical, Oakeshott's ideas on modality make him arguably more liberal than Hayek.

A skeptical defense of free societies rests on acknowledging the epistemic deficiencies observable in human beings. Besides his deep modal skepticism, Oakeshott shares with Hayek and others a view that we simply do not know enough to justify the wielding of vast power or to take on the design of society (Adam Smith, James Madison, and others). Society as a dynamic system is not like other designable systems, even very complex ones. Since individuals respond to circumstances continually and in terms of their understandings, to change those circumstances is to invite a corresponding reassessment of them and a new set of responses. This does not mean change is totally unpredictable, but it does mean that there will always be unforeseen consequences. Also, in attempting to design or reform a society, one is "forming" human lives and not mere matter.

Defining and defending a free society is also a matter of moral humility, which is not to say a doctrine of human nature as bad. Moral humility means accepting limits to one's own powers and being restrained in what one is willing to impose on others through (even lawful) coercion. Moral humility means seeing the inappropriateness of technological metaphor in thinking about ruling. Thus, the skeptical defense of freedom is thoroughly antiutopian or antiperfectionist. It is not a claim that a free society will be the most prosperous society, or the most efficient. It is the recognition that attempts to perfect society, even to make it perfectly free, are inherently problematic.

Epistemic and moral humility lend support to the view that the most appropriate political order is one that leaves human beings as free as possible. This is not because one holds human nature in the abstract to be good. On the contrary, if humans are not good by nature, then it is hard to be optimistic about granting some great power of others. (Miles and Stringham (2014) raise this point). The imperfection of human beings is a reason to limit power, not expand it. But no such doctrine of human nature is really necessary in defining or defending free societies. Epistemic humility means having a readiness to allow human beings to explore, create, and communicate as freely as possible, not because we know this will lead to perfection, or even improvement (a weakness of Mill's view [and possibly Hayek's]), but because their errors and follies are mostly not too harmful.

A fatal confusion between the value of and reasons for freedom is to see beneficial results where people enjoy freedom and convert this into a justification. Good results (social, economic, political, artistic, etc.) often follow freedom; free people in general have more dynamic and prosperous economies, produce splendid art, and engage in exciting scientific discovery.[19] But the skeptical defense of freedom is not consequentialist. This is not only because consequentialism in general has serious flaws, but also because we cannot know enough to be certain that freedom will always and necessarily produce these good outcomes, or produce them for all people in all time frames. Freedom has value in itself, and not as an instrument. It may be that a one-party state enjoys rapid economic growth through aggressive government planning combined with selective liberalization.[20] Such cases will put the consequentially defended free society on the defensive. Moreover, it may be that great art and philosophy can be produced in an atmosphere of repression and censorship. It may even be that a too liberal society lacks impetus to spiritual striving, as Tocqueville, Friedrich Nietzsche and José Ortega y Gasset have argued. (diZerega, 2014, notes Tocqueville's concern with financial oligopoly.) But in such cases, we are being implicitly forced to choose between enjoying freedom or embracing the pursuit of some other goal, be it prosperity, philosophy, or power.

A political skepticism made of epistemic and moral humility results in the judgment that a free society is best, in the limited sense that it is most fit for accommodating the diverse drives and voices of individuals. It does not mean that social harmony is guaranteed, and is consistent with recognizing that the result of maximizing freedom may well be a society that is disorderly, inefficient, unharmonious, and prone to crises and swings in both sentiment and economic indicators, that it may be turbulent, have many cases of unfairness and require continuing and vigilant attention to resolving conflicts and remedying injustice. (Holcombe, 2014, makes a similar point.) A free society is not a magic carpet ride to the Promised Land; it is real, embodied, imperfect human beings, getting along as best they can under conditions they never fully control.

True to that vision of a robustly open social life, liberalism's greatest achievement is to have *liberated spontaneous orders* such as science and the market from epistemic monopolies, including the theocratic state or the expansive secular centralized state or indeed corporate monopolies. Liberality or the modern civil condition is not merely atomistic individuals engaging in voluntary transactions in a mythical and metaphorical marketplace. Individuals are socially embedded and differentiated into multiple personae. Their *interactions* are only partly *exchanges*—in an economically reducible sense. The actions of free individuals are embedded in practices that are not simply markets. Freedom exists at the *nexus* of science, religion, politics, markets, art, and more besides. Libertarians risk losing the legacy of classical liberalism when they advance from the skeptical critique of planning and bureaucracy, to an epistemically imperialistic economism, and thence to a dream of moral and social perfection to be achieved by following purportedly rational principles. Conservatives risk betraying liberty and individuality when they decry atomism, selfishness, and alienation.

On the Plurality of Orders

Like most words in our political vocabulary, "liberty" and "freedom" have several, ambiguous and contested meanings. One widely used meaning is "nondomination" (Pettit). Without endorsing this as the sole or the best meaning, we can use it to see that an important element of freedom is being able to act unrestrictedly, not to be bound. A free society refrains from interfering with its members, and regulation of conduct has to be justified by the highest threshold—undertaking only what is absolutely necessary for political survival and civil order, and acting to offset instances of domination. As important as these considerations are, we argue that to understand the freedom of modern societies, one must appreciate the modal diversity in orientations to the world.

For, there are not merely a wide variety of opinions about the best life for human beings to lead ("experiments in living"), which people should be as free as possible to explore, but many different idioms for conceptualizing, inquiring into, and expressing value and meaning. Science, poetry, history, religion, and more have nonreducible and nonoverlapping viewpoints (Abel, 2009; see also the account of culture as a collection of overlapping spontaneous orders in Camplin, in this volume; and cf. Nell, chapter 6, this volume). However, just as it would be a form of domination to force a person to work in a field not of his or her own choosing, it is a form of domination to force, say, scientific inquiry to serve a technological and commercial master. To say to science, "you may research only what relieves poverty and disease" is to radically curtail the free spirit of inquiry, even if these are worthy goals in their own terms.

Ironically, the modern age has seen the birth of diverse voices of human experience, gradually emancipating themselves from political legend and myth, and has seen the recession of religious and monarchical authority over human conscience. Yet, this same period of liberalizing all forms of experience has also witnessed repeated and persistent attempts to curtail liberty, by making irrelevant demands upon these diverse modes.[21] Thus, science is limited to technological directives. Art is justified only if it serves to expose injustice. History is appreciated only as legend. Perhaps most common is the assertion of the dominance of the practical voice, the insistence that various forms of experience must all serve the general betterment of society or mankind, however defined. Also prevalent are arguments attempting to show the superiority of one voice to all others, to argue, for example, that history is a necessarily impoverished form of science rather than to admit it is simply a form of inquiry that is not relevant to science. The counterclaim, that science itself develops historically and has no "pure" foundation in rational methods is equally absurd.[22]

To be sure, there is also a robust tradition of attempts to distinguish and delineate among the diverse modes of experience. We argue that in such delineation lies an important defense of an important kind of liberty. Since the "self" fragments into modally distinct personae, this recognition of diverse voices or idioms of inquiry is importantly and simultaneously also a recognition of diverse kinds of lives and dispositions. A scientific imperialism (to take but one example) not only offends the pursuit of history but belittles the life and devotions of the historian.

But why would such a broad topic be of interest to libertarians, liberals, or even conservatives? In at least some of its more extreme formulations, libertarianism engages in just this kind of modal imperialism, by elevating the economic idiom to a supreme position, and by embracing a rationalistic style leading to dogmatic assertions about the one proper form and purpose of political life. And in these matters, some conservatives ally themselves with libertarians, or share their views, at least on economic matters.

Since at least Adam Smith's "invisible hand," economic activity has been a powerful metaphor for broader social integration, and society itself has very often been seen as a vast "marketplace." Economists are prone, like any scientists, to be in love with their way of seeing the world, and aware of the insights their inquiries have achieved. But also, like any true scientist, they are usually aware of the limits of their knowledge. It is usually popularizers who do the crassest reductionism, although even the best economists sometimes become prosyletic. A major temptation to overstating the claims of economics comes from the fact that a very large proportion of the activities of many people are in fact economic—making, trading, getting, selling. But even if economics can account for a majority of mankind's occupations and preoccupations, it does not follow that all activities are economic in nature.[23]

Further, it has long been recognized that the conception of self and society rooted in nothing but bare consumption of goods is empty, even without invoking religious arguments about ultimate meaning. What Oakeshott has called the "danse macabre of wants and satisfactions" has been noted by others:

> To paraphrase David Riesman and José Ortega y Gasset, there is no lonelier crowd than the mass man, the anonymous consumer who has exhausted the roster of "need-satisfactions," as the expression goes, whether the latter can be the consumption of the manifold goods of a sophisticated consumer society or the services of the four hundred or so different schools of psychotherapy. (1991: 299)

Much that is free is not exchange. Even if activities can be said to have costs and involve trade-offs, this does not mean the activity is for the sake of those things. A day of surfing does, practically speaking, take one away from the economically valuable effort of building one's company's website, and can be said to impose a "cost," but it is not a business expense. Nor is the surfing redeemed by contributing to relaxation, which supports more focused work. First, the "down time" view fails to distinguish surfing from sleeping pills. Second, it totally misses the point of surfing to justify it (or criticize it) in these economic terms. It is like feeing disappointed that the Boston Red Sox did not try for a field goal to win the game.[24] Similarly, it may be denied that friendship is an end in itself, and asserted that it can be understood "economically" as a trade-off between professional activities and enjoyment of another's company. Or it can be seen under the guise of "useful friendships" based on favors and mutual aid. But the noninstrumental enjoyment of another's company is a rejection of the entire worldview of economic trade-offs, and is not reducible to it. An economist can understand the activity of friendship in economic terms, but in doing so, he has stripped it of the meaning friendship has for friends. It is like understanding sex as a form of exercise, or marriage as a contract for sex. To understand humans as self-interpreting beings, one has to understand their self-understandings, what activities and relationships mean to them.

Applied to an entire society, these kinds of *reading into* can be very distorting. Instead of recognizing a society as an association of human beings relating to one another in a multitude of different ways, the economic idiom favored by libertarians (and many liberals and conservatives) means that all noneconomic activity is going to be understood in a distorted fashion. When this happens, it is easy to lose sight of noneconomic (or even antieconomic) justifications, for, say, law. For instance, all laws have some kinds of substantive impacts. Even the most neutral, "rules of the road" types of regulations imply that, for example, in the United States, shops along the right side of the roadway will be easier to enter for cars bound in one direction, while in the United Kingdom, it will be the shops on the left side that receive the traffic from the same direction of travel.[25] Oversensitivity to the economic impacts of laws and regulations could lead to the view that all laws impose inefficiencies and should be eliminated. A corrective program of rooting out inefficiency and malinvestment can flip into a utopian anarchism. A classically liberal position admits that some inefficiency may simply have to be borne. It would be wise to avoid this as much as possible—and here, libertarians' diagnoses of the cost of public policies are very helpful. But what is possible or desirable is largely circumstantially determined and cannot be decided on the basis of pure reason alone. As we saw above, both libertarianism and "high" liberalism suffer from rationalistic visions of grandeur. But their principles rarely if ever meet the test of practical plausibility. The empirical evidence for such ideological visions is spotty at best.

The bigger point, however, is that if we take an economic modeler's perspective on the whole of society, then it will seem appropriate to conceive the values of economic models—efficiency, equilibrium, productivity, prosperity, and so forth—as the cardinal values of the society. What works brilliantly as a social science and as a form of public policy critique may work less well as an account of all human social relations.

So-called "conservatives," on the other hand, may be taken to task for not appreciating the tension between the market and their preferred sociopolitical values. This is a point also made by Hayek long ago. The dynamism of markets can undercut traditions, true. But this point is ambiguous. It is also possible that markets can sustain traditions. Certainly there is no shortage of turkeys for sale in the United States every November, or rosaries in Rome every Easter.[26] The net effect of markets on traditions is bound to be mixed and ambiguous. More to the point, the conservative politician who embraces economic growth and rising income as his political aims, and promises voters he will enhance their standard of living is making several false steps. First, he is making promises that in the nature of things will be very difficult if not impossible to fulfill. Next, he is fundamentally in agreement with the "high" liberal or progressive about ends—full employment, a comfortable life for all—but disagrees only about means. Third, like the "high" liberal or progressive, he holds (perhaps unwittingly) that political life is the ordering of human affairs in relation to a telos. While he may speak of liberty, his outlook on the role of government has actually turned in a quite illiberal direction. Some conservatives seem oblivious of adopting a rationalistic and teleocratic view that they as conservatives should reject, by promoting a substantive theory of the human good.[27]

On offer is *not* an antimarket critique. On the contrary, we wish to preserve the integrity of the market, and also science and other forms of experience, but it needs to be understood that each mode has its own criteria of objectivity, standards, and teleology, and cannot be answerable to (or reducible to) another mode's teleology or metric. Furthermore, it is the sine qua non of the liberal condition that there will always be tensions between orders: to reduce one realm to another is thus antiliberal (Marsh and Hardwick, 2013).

Conclusion

In summary: we are defending freedom, noting that as the idea of freedom has spread and the world has seen increasing liberalization, the understanding of freedom, individuality, and the basis of a free society seems to have become more muddled and ambiguous. Libertarians, "high liberals," and conservatives all defend liberty, yet they all tend to be rationalistic and teleological. Libertarians also tend to defend a very narrow theory of freedom as "choice" or "voluntariness" or "voluntary exchange," while conservatives tend to disparage individualism and confuse it with atomism. Individuality is really only possible within traditions, practices, languages, communities. It is also the case that these traditions cannot move, grow, or change without individual initiative and free action. So the juxtaposition of individual and community that is a staple of much modern discussion is simply misplaced. A distinction can be drawn, of course, and for some purposes needs to be drawn, but it is more a matter of degree than an ontological imperative. A key basis for a *classical liberalism* worthy of the name is skepticism—moral and epistemic. We recognize that there are limits to what can be achieved in the actual world as opposed to the world of abstract theorizing, and that political change involves more than the administration of things—it involves the reformation and alteration of settled patterns of conduct that have proven their worth to those living in them. We further recognize that human reason is embedded in tradition, is imperfect, and is limited in ways that make large-scale social planning impossible. Finally, freedom needs to be understood as more than atomistic marketplace behavior. As important as markets are, and as much good as they deliver, human interaction is richer and more diverse than commercial exchange. Also, there are a number of independent, modally distinct orientations to the world, the flourishing of which is vital to both the "conversation of mankind" and the enjoyment of our nature as free, self-interpreting beings. Any view, economic or otherwise, that fails to appreciate this modal diversity will distort our understanding of both human freedom and society.

NOTES

1. See, for example, Brennan, 2012. Of interest, he draws a slightly different distinction. According to a review by John McCloskey, "Brennan claims there have been three kinds of libertarians: classical liberals, such as Adam Smith, John Locke, F. A. Hayek, Milton Friedman, and America's founders; 'hard libertarians' such as Ayn Rand, Murray Rothbard, and Nozick; and neoclassical liberals, such as Brennan, Tomasi, and others of the new Rawlsian doctrine. The first group were defenders of liberty but not as doctrinaire as the hard libertarians, Brennan says. And those hard libertarians of the late 1900s, he assures his readers, are now only a fringe part of libertarianism. (Older libertarians have been appalled to be so marginalized.) Libertarians that are now the mainline, Brennan reports, are not dogmatically committed to the non-aggression principle. They defend their commitment to free-market institutions because these institutions are the ones that best 'serve the interests of the poor and least advantaged.' The new mainstream libertarians are not ideologically opposed to, say, government schools or social safety nets" (McCaskey, 2014). Also, Palmer (2013) suggests libertarianism coalesces around support for individual rights, spontaneous order, and limited government, thus falling closer to the "classical liberal" tradition rather than "hard libertarian" views.
2. It must be conceded that the use of the term "conservative: also has an indexical sense, i.e., relative to a context. So, for example, anyone who wished (or still wishes) to preserve the essentials of Communist Party rule, would on these terms, be deemed a conservative.
3. Like Oakeshott, Walker Percy notes that the categories liberal and conservative have long since been emptied of any meaning (Percy 1991: 58, 248, 416).
4. Holcombe (2014) makes the important point that spontaneous orders can be improved by both "codification" and "design." As an additional consideration, Oakeshott asks whether that design, e.g., reflective political activity, is (a) based upon abstract principles detached from historic experience, or grounded in concrete considerations and (b) aimed toward a telos that requires the conscription of societal resources on a large scale, or respects genuine voluntariness.
5. Oakeshott famously articulated his self-ascribed conservatism, not as a creed nor as a doctrine, but as a disposition. Having a conservative disposition in terms of character or personality traits has nothing, logically or even

psychologically, to do with whether one is a conservative in politics. The two can combine, but this is utterly contingent.

6. Percy writes: "*Political* conservatism is neither sinful nor illegal—though sometimes one wonders if liberals don't think it is" (1991: 92, ital. added).
7. Hayek's celebrated critique of the notion of "social justice"—that when transactions are made under abstract general laws, necessary for freedom, they will be just—means that since justice only holds between individuals, there can be no such thing as "social justice" between groups and classes.
8. Block prizes himself on his logic, but his defense of slavery is patently illogical. He rejects contracts for murder on grounds that such a contract involves an agreement to harm another. But in his defense of the slavery contract, he argues that the person who enters the contract is not the same as the person who lives under it later. "First, there is a 'person' who is able to make contracts. . . . Second, at an entirely different time period, there is this slave, who is no longer a (legal) person." And he refers to two distinct "persons" existing at "t1" and "t2" (2011: 549). Never mind that this entirely begs the question of how, and more precisely, whether it is even possible, that "person at t1" turned herself into "person at t2." It is just this possibility of transforming oneself freely into a nonfree being that is at issue. Block assumes it as an accomplished fact, making his argument circular. He does that to avoid the classical liberal argument against a self-refuting exercise of freedom. But in thus splitting the person, he creates the logical equivalent of the murder-for-hire contract, in which the earlier version of oneself is a different person contracting with another to harm a third party, the later version of oneself. He also argues that the person entering into slavery could be doing so to help a sick child in need of care. There is the problem here of genuine consent—if one consents under the kind of financial pressure that Block's own example imagines, then it is not clear that the agent is acting in their own interests, or why a simple working relationship would not suffice—selling one's labor, instead of alienating one's basic liberty. Further, Block does not consider how helpful it will be to the child if the parent has sold herself (Blocks' example is feminine) into slavery. Presumably, a slavery contract can include favorable terms allowing visitation, and a continued right to parent the child, without interfering in the slave's duties. It really seems the point of an argument like Block's is the old sophistical one of trying to show the absurdities one can get some to accept by way of "arguments."
9. See Oakeshott 1975a, especially the "Introduction to Leviathan," for a brilliant counterview.
10. A most penetrating and sustained analysis of the concept of the self can be found in Percy 1983.
11. Consider the doyen of situated theorists of cognitive science expressing the very insights that Hayek and Oakeshott (and Percy) share: "This power of culture and language to shape human subjectivity and experience belongs not simply to the genetic constitution of the individual, but to the generative constitution of the intersubjective community.

Individual subjectivity is from the outset intersubjectivity, as a result of the communally handed down norms, conventions, artifacts, and cultural traditions in which the individual is always already embedded. Thus the internalization of joint attention into symbolic representations is not simply an ontogenetic phenomenon, but a historical and cultural one" (Thompson, 2007: 409).

12. Denis, in this volume, traces Hayek's efforts to explain both the individual's action (which is a matter of *Verstehen*) and the unintended results of many individuals' actions.
13. Although Adam Smith's *Wealth of Nations* (WN) is typically invoked as providing the conceptual validation for capitalism and laissez-faire, a close reading of both the *Wealth of Nations* and his more foundational book, *Theory of Moral Sentiments* (TMS), gives cold comfort to ideologues, dissolving the perceived tension in trying to reconcile the view of human nature expounded in TMS (sympathy and benevolence) and the view of human nature expounded in WN (self-interest). See Hardwick and Marsh, forthcoming.
14. See Bellah et al. 1996. The authors' interesting argument about the influence of the language of individualism aside, the main problem for them is the loneliness that (purportedly) comes from a lack of "vision" and "common culture." Also see Putnam, 1995, who enlists Tocqueville in the cause of enterprise association: what will remedy the ills of individualism are "collective action," "cooperation for mutual benefit," greater "social capital," etc.
15. The above section on nomocracy and teleocracy is adapted from Abel 1995.
16. The right of emigration is embedded in the UN Declaration of Rights (Article 13), but this is a marginal phenomenon. Short of emigration, an individual is indeed bound inescapably to the laws of his domicile. Other exceptional cases like diplomatic immunity only support the point.
17. This theme is pursued more fully in Abel 2014. See also, Nell, chapter 6, in this volume, who notes how planning society leads to "planning the individual." While this may happen in any "instrumental order" or telic association, the right of exit and the state's right to compel are crucial considerations.
18. Stringham and Miles (2014) make a bold effort to vitiate the state's authority claims by highlighting the sordid genealogy of acquired power. However, to limit power by denying legitimacy is inherently risky—unless one is an all-out anarchist who believes order can emerge without at least occasional compulsion. Oakeshott's civil association gives a reason for understanding how long-established legal orders (even if sordid in origin) may win the assent of those subject to them. See also Bylund (2014), who explores whether and how firms within markets possess authority. Oakeshott's critique of teleocracy helps clarify why it is problematic to conceive, as Vladimir Lenin did, an entire society as a factory.
19. Cowen 2004 is full of fine examples of the superabundance of "goods" of all kinds produced under conditions of freedom. This is, of course, a regularity claim, not a necessitarianism claim.

20. The obvious contemporary case is China. The sycophantic and obsequious praise China has attracted from some pundits should be alarming to anyone who values freedom, since China's feats of growth have been converted into an argument for more government intrusions and control in free societies. The argument—right or wrong on its merits in interpreting China—values growth over freedom.
21. Kuehn's (2014) account of different theories of unemployment is a case study of economics trying to free itself from practical concerns and achieve an idiomatically distinct and consistent voice. Also, Camplin's effort to build from Turner's view of diverse economies to diverse "spontaneous orders" would be encouraged by Oakeshott's differentiation of experience into distinct modes. See Camplin, this volume.
22. The attack upon history was famously put forward in Karl Popper's *Poverty of Historicism*; the critical studies movement, neo-Marxists, sociology of knowledge camps have had their day asserting that everything is political; and Thomas Kuhn single-handedly produced cosmic quantities of mental fog with his historicist account of scientific paradigm shifts.
23. Cumbers (2014) complains of the neoliberal orthodoxy, but developing a form of market socialism remains a fundamentally economic project, whereas Oakeshott's pluralism is rooted in epistemology. Also, it is hard to see how a project to "rethink the relations between economic democracy, markets, ownership, and planning" avoids the pitfalls of rationalism and teleocracy, although Cumbers is aware of the need to do so (Cf. Nell, 2014).
24. For those not familiar with American sports: the Red Sox are a baseball team, and the field goal is a way of scoring in "football."
25. The fact of a substantive impact would not make the law "purposive" in Oakeshott's sense. It would still be an "adverbial" condition observed in conduct because it does not seek to dictate a specific outcome, like visiting a shop or a shopping area. The effect of the law is unavoidable, but it still leaves agents free to stop along the high street or head out past the M25 for some hillwalking, as it suits them.
26. Scruton (2007: 219–220) makes the point that "Those who believe that social order demands constraints on the market are right. But in a true spontaneous order the constraints are already there, in the form of customs, laws, and morals."
27. Percy (1985: 23) notes, "This is the radical right wing which has corrupted the whole conservative tradition. They use the words *conservative* and *constitutional*. They have appropriated these words and the have prostituted the whole tradition. They are not conservatives."

REFERENCES

Abel, Corey. 1995. "Michael Oakeshott's Liberalism: The Epistemology of Experience and the Morality of Individualism." PhD diss., University of Chicago.

———. 2005. "Appropriating Aristotle." In Corey Abel (ed.), *The Intellectual Legacy of Michael Oakeshott*, 37–60. Exeter: Imprint Academic.

———. 2009. "Oakeshottian Modes at the Crossroads of the Evolution Debates." *Zygon: Journal of Science & Religion,* 44(1): 197–222.

———. 2014. "The Instrumental Idiom in American Politics: The 'City on the Hill' As A Spontaneous Order." *Cosmos + Taxis: Studies in Emergent Order and Organization,* 3(1): forthcoming.

Bellah, Robert N. et al. 1996. *Habits of the Heart: Individualism and Commitment in American Life.* updated ed. Berkeley: University of California Press.

Block, Walter. 2011. "Illiberal Libertarians: Why Libertarianism is not a Liberal View, and a Good Thing, Too." *Journal of Libertarian Studies,* 2: 537–580.

Brennan, Jason. 2012. *Libertarianism: What Everyone Needs to Know.* Oxford: Oxford University Press.

Callahan, Eugene. 2013. "Liberty Versus Libertarianism." *Politics, Philosophy & Economics,* 12(1): 48–67.

Carson, Kevin. 2014. "Economic Calculation under Capitalist Central Planning." In Guinevere Liberty Nell (ed.), *Austrian Theory and Economic Organization,* pp. 57–96. New York: Palgrave Macmillan.

Clark, Andy. 1997. *Being There: Putting Brain, Body, and World Together Again.* Cambridge: MIT Press.

Coats, Wendell John. 1985. "Michael Oakeshott as Liberal Theorist." *Canadian Journal of Political Science,* 18: 773–787.

———. 1992. "Some Correspondence between Oakeshott's 'Civil Condition' and the Republican Tradition." *Political Science Reviewer,* 21: 99–115.

Cowen, Tyler. 2004. *Creative Destruction: How Globalization Is Changing the World's Cultures.* Princeton: Princeton University Press.

Cumbers, Andrew. 2014. "Responding to Hayek from the Left: Beyond Market Socialism on the Path to a Radical Economic Democracy." In Guinevere Liberty Nell (ed.), *Austrian Theory and Economic Organization,* pp. 177–198. New York: Palgrave Macmillan.

diZerega, Gus. 2013. "Turning the Tables: The Pathologies and Unrealized Promise of Libertarianism." In Georgia Kelly (ed.), *Uncivil Liberties: Deconstructing Libertarianism.* Sonoma: Praxis Peace Institute.

———. 2014. "Contract, Freedom, and Flourishing: The Implications of Spain's Mondragon Cooperatives." In Guinevere Liberty Nell (ed.), *Austrian Theory and Economic Organization,* pp. 123–146. New York: Palgrave Macmillan.

Franco, Paul. 1990. "Michael Oakeshott as Liberal Theorist." *Political Theory,* 18: 411–436.

Freeden, Michael. 1994. "Political Concepts and Ideological Morphology." *Journal of Political Philosophy,* 2(2): 140–164.

Freeman, Samuel. 2002. "Illiberal Libertarians: Why Libertarianism Is not a Liberal View." *Philosophy and Public Affairs,* 30(2): 105–151.

———. 2011. "Capitalism in the Classical and High Liberal Traditions." *Social Philosophy and Policy Foundation,* 28(2): 19–55.

Friedman, Jeffrey. 1989. "The New Consensus: The Fukayama Thesis." *Critical Review,* 4(3): 373–410.

Hardwick, David, and Leslie Marsh. 2012. "Clash of the Titans: When the Market and Science Collide." In *Experts and Epistemic Monopolies, Advances in Austrian Economics* 17: 37–60. Bingley, UK: Emerald.

———. 2013. "Science, the Market and Iterative Knowledge." *Studies in Emergent Order* 5: 26–44.

———. 2014. *Propriety and Prosperity: New Studies on the Philosophy of Adam Smith*. Basingstoke: Palgrave Macmillan, forthcoming.

Hayek, Friedrich A. 1960. "Why I Am Not a Conservative." In *The Constitution of Liberty*, pp. 397–411. Chicago: University of Chicago Press.

Holcombe, Randall G. 2014. "Improving Spontaneous Orders." In Guinevere Liberty Nell (ed.), *Austrian Theory and Economic Organization*, pp. 9–28. New York: Palgrave Macmillan.

Hutto, Daniel D. 2005. "Knowing What? Radical Versus Conservative Enactivism." *Phenomenology and the Cognitive Sciences*, 4(4): 389–405.

Kakathas, Chandran. (2009). "Two Constructions of Libertarianism." *Libertarian Papers*, 1(11): 1–13.

Kuehn, Daniel. 2014. "The Problem of Unemployment When Markets Clear." In Guinevere Liberty Nell (ed.), *Austrian Theory and Economic Organization*, pp. 29–54. New York: Palgrave Macmillan.

Marsh, Leslie. 2010. "Ryle and Oakeshott on the Know-how/Know-that Distinction. In Corey Abel (ed.), *The Meanings of Michael Oakeshott's Conservatism*, 143–160. Exeter: Imprint Academic.

———. 2012. "Hayek and Oakeshott: Situating the Mind." In Paul Franco and Leslie Marsh (eds.), *A Companion to Michael Oakeshott*, 248–267. University Park: Penn State University Press.

———. 2013. "Mindscapes and Landscapes: Hayek and Simon on Cognitive Extension." In Roger Frantz and Robert Leeson (eds.), *Hayek and Behavioural Economics*, 248–267. Basingstoke: Palgrave Macmillan.

McCaskey, John P. 2014. "New Libertarians: New Promoters of a Welfare State," http://www.johnmccaskey.com/joomla/index.php/blog/71-new-libertarians.

Miles, Caleb J., and Stringham, Edward Peter. 2014. "Eliminating the Perceived Legitimacy of the State." In Guinevere Liberty Nell (ed.), *Austrian Theory and Economic Organization*, pp. 147–174. New York: Palgrave Macmillan.

Nell, Guinevere Liberty. 2014. "The Post-Austrian School and the New Market Socialism." In Guinevere Liberty Nell (ed.), *Austrian Theory and Economic Organization*, pp. 197–238. New York: Palgrave Macmillan.

Oakeshott, Michael. 1975. *On Human Conduct*. Oxford: Clarendon Press.

———. 1975a. *Hobbes on Civil Association*. Indianapolis: Liberty Fund.

———. 1983. *On History and Other Essays*. Oxford: Basil Blackwell.

———. 1991. *Rationalism in Politics and Other Essays*, new and expanded edition, ed. Timothy Fuller. Indianapolis: Liberty Press.

Palmer, Tom G., ed. 2013. *Why Liberty: Your Life, Your Choices, Your Future*. Ottawa, IL: Jameson Books.

Percy, Walker. 1983. *Lost in the Cosmos: The Last Self-Help Book*. New York: Farrar Straus & Giroux.

———. 1985. *Conversations with Walker Percy*, eds. Lewis A. Lawson and Victor A. Kramer. Jackson, MS: University Press of Mississippi.

———. 1991. *Signposts in a Strange Land*, ed. with an intro. by Patrick Samway. New York: Picador.

Putnam, Robert. 1995. "Bowling Alone." *Journal of Democracy* 6(1): 65–78.

Sandel, Michael J. 1984. *Liberalism and Its Critics*. New York: New York University Press.

Scruton, Roger. 2007. "Hayek and Conservatism." In Edward Feser (ed.), *The Cambridge Companion to Hayek*, 208–231. Cambridge: Cambridge University Press.

Swanson Judith. 2013. "Prudence and Human Conduct: A Comparison of Aristotle and Oakeshott." In Michael Henkel and Oliver W. Lembcke (ed.), *Praxis und Politik—Michael Oakeshott im Dialog*, 21–38. Tuebingen: Mohr Siebeck.

Taylor, Charles. 1985. *Philosophy and the Human Sciences: Philosophical Papers 2*. Cambridge: Cambridge University Press.

———. 1989. *Sources of the Self: The Making of the Modern Identity*. Cambridge: Harvard University Press.

Thompson, Evan. 2007. *Mind in Life: Biology, Phenomenology, and the Sciences of the Mind*. Cambridge: Harvard University Press.

CHAPTER 6

The Internal and the External Freedoms: How Hayek's Ideas on Mind and Society Can Help Achieve Marx's Utopian Dreams

Guinevere Liberty Nell

Introduction

It is now accepted by most economists that economic planning is inefficient and authoritarian—hindering freedom of the individual—although many believe that this would not be true if the people were enlightened and altruistic, having changed human nature. Although freedom of speech and thought have been constrained in planned economies, the arguments for the inevitability of this outcome often hinge upon the state's desire to retain power. This is the common assumption regarding the reason for the criminalization of consciousness—or preferences or perspectives—the prosecution of "thought-crimes," which has occurred in "fundamentalist" planned economies. However, based on Austrian theory or upon economic history, one can argue that planning of the economy *necessarily* leads to "planning" of the individual.

A given system's effect upon the individual's power (magnitude, strength, and flexibility) of free choice must be examined, including whether his or her choice is determined by the system's forces more than the individual's preferences, The endogenous effect of the system upon preferences and actions must be considered, along with its effect on the psychological development of the individual and the psychology and beliefs of the society as a whole.

The evolution of a society's culture is dependent on: its institutions, their effect upon the behavior and preferences of the individuals in the system, and the individuals' subsequent effect on the system's institutions (at least in a democracy). This cyclical process is described by Ludwig von Mises in *Human Action.* Writing about the interaction between the individual and society, he argues that, "the controversy whether the whole or its parts are logically prior is vain. Logically the notions of a whole and its parts are correlative. As logical concepts they are both apart from time" (Mises, 1966 [1949]: 42).In each distinct system, the evolutionary process will have different specific rules upon which selection acts, and hence different forces affecting selection, producing differing results. One system may be driven by personal monetary gain (economic power and "materialism"), while another is driven by power, or pride and prestige, for example. The cultural evolution within a set of institutions could theoretically induce a change in "human nature" just as Karl Marx and Vladimir Lenin argued, but without the imposition of institutions that may have caused their failure (Nell, 2014a).

Psychological development of the mind that influences an individual's preferences and beliefs will be developed as a reflection of the society in which that mind resides. F. A. Hayek was an early advocate of the neural network approach to understanding human consciousness (Gauss, 2006), and he argues that the mind is a complex system or "spontaneous order" (Hayek, 1978a: 250). The complex system of the mind, like the complex system of the market and all complex systems, requires a free area in order to develop "naturally" and evolve toward a well-functioning system. Hayek's arguments on complexity and planning can be extended to his cognitive development theories and offer a way to relate the arguments regarding the internal (psychological) and external (social) systems.[1]

One obvious implication is the effect of a planned system upon psychological freedom and individualism within a planned economy. However, because the power to act upon free thoughts and preferences in a market system relies upon the power to act in the market system, and to demonstrate preferences (which requires money), a laissez-faire system may not offer the individual the most psychological freedom; furthermore, noneconomic preferences may not be fulfilled, and preferences may be affected by the system itself (see also Nell, 2013). Finally, what about the psychological desire for community? A purely free-market system may not fulfill this desire as much as some other, more communitarian, systems would, for example. If individuals were more enlightened, perhaps a more enlightened system would be possible, allowing both freedom of the individual and a more communal society.

HAYEK AND THE MIND AS A COMPLEX SYSTEM

A complex system is made up of a large number of interacting elements. A spontaneous order emerges from these interactions (Hayek, 1973). Hayek contrasts the spontaneous ordering of "life, mind, and society" (1973: 41), with the "constructivistic" (1978b: 3) fallacy that complex systems such as these must be centrally ordered. This is the same fallacy, he argues, as William Paley's "argument from design" (Popper, 1987: 13), which argues that the complexity of life, mind, and society are so great that a creator must be behind them. Complex systems, whether of society or of mind, can emerge spontaneously, and evolution can bring about greater complexity than a single mind (or a single party line) has yet to produce. (Of course, arguably Hayek was wrong to consider central planning as necessarily representing a single mind or set of choices. Even in the Soviet Union there was a certain amount of feedback from below that modified the plan as it was carried out [Nell, 2010].)

Hayek spoke about many complex systems in the social sphere of life, including the market, civil society, and language. He also investigated human behavior and cognition. Hayek's work on cognition and behavior informs his analysis of markets and price, and his theory of civil society. Hayek describes a neural network connectionist philosophy of the emergence of the mind (Dempsey, 1996). There are neural connections that are made in the infant, as it senses the world around it and makes abstract connections between sensed objects. Combinations of impulses and connections between them contribute to larger networks, or "patterns," and a "density" of neural connections. Each neuron gradually acquires a defined place in the system of neural connections. This is how a view of the world and an identity are formed within a person's mind as she develops. An infant has a "much thinner net of ordering relations" than an adult (1978c: p44). This corresponds to many of the psychological descriptions of ego development (Cook-Greuter, 2000).

This "connectionist" view also informs theory on how memory and understanding of the world can be faulty. For example, according to the connectionist view, networks of experiences are often related by common sensory data that allow us to form patterns and abstract concepts from sensory images. This may also affect memory retrieval in the following way. When we remember an experience—for example, we remember the last time that we saw a friend—we will remember it in context. The memory may be that we had dinner, and this dinner was, for example, Indian food. However, if we enjoy Indian food, the memory of this enjoyment may be connected to a pattern of positive neural clusterings that relate to this (good food) experience, rather than to experiences with the friend. If this occurs, the retrieval of memories relating to the friend, when triggered by this particular memory, may be more positive than if retrieved when triggered by a different memory of time spent with him or her.

This may explain why sometimes it can be difficult to accurately determine an overall impression of someone or something. If we cannot retrieve all of our memories of a person at once, the group that we retrieve may depend upon the triggering memory that allows us to pull up a cluster of memories. If we use this cluster to take an overall impression of our estimation of the person or thing, we be may be using a biased group. The judgment then depends upon the particular cluster. Not only may the most recent experience stand out in our minds and cloud the overall impression, but also, ceteris paribus, the cluster may be biased by the triggering memory.

This may contribute to easily biased views, as we listen to those with whom we seek group identification, and fall for statistical fallacies, groupthink, and irrational beliefs. This can explain some of the ability of advertising to fool people. It also may explain the positive memories some individuals have of the past, even when that past was "“objectively worse” than the present, if, for example, there were some warm memories of communal gatherings that are linked to the otherwise negative aspects of the system.

KEEPING THE MIND OPEN: THE ECONOMY

Although freedom of speech and thought have been constrained in planned economies, explanations for the cause of this outcome often hinge upon a political incentive to retain power, rather than upon a theory that they follow directly from planning itself. However, planned economies have often required individuals to conform to the plan, hindering their freedom of thought, since the plan was unable to fulfill the actual desires of the people (Nell, 2010; 2014a).

Either planners must be able to fulfill the actual desires of the people or the people must be influenced to desire what is produced by the plan. Aldous Huxley's novel *Brave New World* (1969) includes an extreme case of the latter: individuals are born and raised to play certain roles, and the state intercepts people's preferences during sleep, hence planners are able to ensure their production fulfills the demand of the people. In real-world planned economies, preferences were influenced by state-advertising, propaganda, indoctrination, and intimidation. Although advertisers in a market economy influence people to demand their product, planners may even more forcefully mold people to their wishes. Planners have incentive to influence the thinking and desires of the individual to coincide with the plan, essentially planning people's personalities and preferences in addition to their choices.

The implication of the argument that planning reduces economic freedom and therefore individual freedom, is that planning of the economy leads to planning of the individual. This argument explains the prevalence of thought crimes in "fundamentalist" planned economies. Economic planning imposes the economic plan upon the individual's life and mind. Individuals in socialist societies are popularly depicted, with good reason, as having a mentality restricted by socialist ideology (see, for example, the film *Silk Stockings*). This is not only due to propaganda, but it arises from the requirements of the planners to set a course for individual lives and minds that corresponds to the plan for society.

In planned economic systems, leaders have always demanded unity of will both inside and outside of the political sphere (the party). This is no coincidence: unity of will is necessary in order for planning to produce the desired outcome. While in a market society bad luck might leave an individual hungry, and the oppression of the strong can keep the weak in poverty, in a society of common ownership and shared construction, socialists argued, no worker (or sick or disabled person) would have to be left behind. However, this outcome would depend upon the people's agreeing upon a *common* plan of production and uniting behind it.[2]

In order that there not be contradictions between personal and social interests, this common plan of production must be agreed to by each individual. Just as an individual in a market society might find a price ruinous, an individual in a planned society might find his part in the plan ruinous. Bukharin (1921: chapter 2, section c) seems not to have considered this possibility when he writes,

> Let us suppose that we have a little society or circle of persons who have organized to sing together. All propose the same goal for themselves, propose to solve the questions involved, to evaluate the difficulties with which they are faced, in short, they make resolutions in common and carry them out in common.

In another utopian example, he writes that "Five men resolve to lift a stone together. Alone, none of them could lift it; together, they do so without difficulty." Bukharin concludes that "The general resolution does not differ by a hair's breadth from the desire of each individual. On the contrary, it aids in the realization of this desire" (1921: chapter 2, section c). However, Bukharin's examples implicitly assume a common will: the people "have organized to sing together," or "resolve to lift a stone together." If instead they have *been organized* by some central authority, there is no clear reason to believe they unanimously favor the decision. Lenin always argued for implementing the decision of *the majority of class-conscious workers*. Yet, if the goal were decided by majority rule, the dissenting minority would have their desires and plans frustrated, and Bukharin's conclusion would not be warranted.

The people must agree to the common plan of production, for the society to function well. The people must in fact actively, physically and psychologically, support the plan. If there is disagreement with the production plan, the good outcome cannot be ensured. In fact, then the minority might be worse off. If some individuals wanted to lift a stone and others wanted to leave the stone in place, one cannot conclude that all would be made better off by coming together to lift it. In that case, some may be made the slaves of others. In order to be sure of a good outcome, unanimity of choice is required (for more on this see Nell, 2014b).

Yet, it is not only in a planned society that an individual's mind may be planned or forced into certain constraints or in a certain direction. Religious societies that are not economically planned may direct an individual psychologically. The freedom of the complex system of the mind requires that the individual is not coerced psychologically by a central plan, *or by the traditions* of the social or economic sphere. He or she should not feel forced to plan his or her life according to specified expectations or rules, and should not be limited by narrow rationality from experiencing broader mental awareness. Mental freedom, the full scope for the development of the individual's mind, requires an environment of social *and* economic freedom.

McCann (2002) describes Hayek's assertion that we have a moral duty that is "inherent in our constitution, part of our socially-embedded nature," but that our social duty to be moral is not coercion, despite the fact that we may face punishment if we do not live up to expectations. He quotes Hayek, saying that "It is part of the ordinary nature of men . . . and one of the main conditions of their happiness that they make the welfare of other people their chief aim," and says,

> Yet the acceptance of personal responsibility and the feeling of obligation is nonetheless a free act, and not the product of a coercive state, demanding conformity to a social norm. Actions are free to be taken so long as one is willing to bear the consequences of those actions, including the onus of social ostracism and the potential loss of personal advantage deriving from the inability to achieve desired objectives. The important point is that personal responsibility born from moral duty is inextricably entwined with free, individual action in a liberal society. (McCann, 2002: 78)

This is a debatable distinction: If it is coercion to have to pay employees the minimum wage or else pay a fine or face other punishment, why is it not coercion if one has to act a certain way or else face the punishment of social ostracism? Whether it is the morality of communism, a religious society, or the individualistic morality of market societies, it may be as coercive as legal mandates if social ostracism is the punishment for disobeying. It is almost always the case that "Actions are free to be taken so long as one is willing to bear the consequences of those actions," if in this you include the consequences of going to prison or being tortured or killed. This is not freedom—this is coercion. And complete social ostracism as a punishment might be as bad as prison, and is certainly worse than a fine; so, social coercion can be as bad or worse than much of what is categorized as coercion by Austrians and libertarians.

Norms, as Robert Heilbroner (1986: 59) points out in his discussion of Adam Smith's Theory of Moral Sentiments, are modes of behavior "calculated to win approval," and helping to make the individual worthy of such approval, and are hence about normalizing the individuals' behavior, or offering people a standard of "normal" that is moral. According to Heilbroner, Smith's idea of virtue is "not reducible to fixed rules" because it "is always mediated by the empathetic properties of human understanding." This describes an evolutionary process: Morality, and the norms and culture that govern it, evolves with social interaction, in which individuals learn from their perception of others' experiences in addition to their own. Subjectivity (perspective), rationality, and emotion or solidarity (enhancing the experience of empathy) must all play a role in this process.

Heilbroner (1986: 59) criticizes Smith's argument for not explaining how or why humankind rises from "mere expediency of seeking praise to the genuine morality of seeking to be praiseworthy." Yet, this can easily be explained by the evolutionary process: Although individuals may start by faking morality in order to gain approval, it may be a case of "fake it til you make it" because those who—on occasion, at first, and then increasingly often—truly aim to *be* moral will likely do the best job of "faking it." The selection process in social evolution would thereby lead to a more truly moral people.

Any external command order will want to limit the internal (individual) spontaneous order in order to control it, and so will tend to limit speech (which aids learning), drug use, and free religious or metaphysical inquiry; but, even a system that does not explicitly attempt to plan the individual's cognition, choices, or preferences may affect them through the forces that are most powerfully driving the system and therefore that most affect the spontaneous order of the mind. The various spontaneous orders within a society necessarily affect each other (see Camplin, this volume), and therefore a powerful force such as consumerism will affect the feedback cycle of the internal spontaneous order of the mind.

Choice is partly determined, or at least influenced by, the system's forces in addition to the individual's preferences.

Hayek recognized the ineffability of the external and internal complex systems, outside of subjective relativism (Feser, 2006: 292–293) and the axiom of action (praxeology). Hayek did not believe that introspection was enough to know the mind; as we shall discuss below he did not believe the mind could be fully known (see also Feser, 2006: 293, 298), yet is this not precisely what is required for the axiom of action and the assumption of a fixed self-interested human nature?

Hayek argues that the rules governing thought cannot be known and that we must "just act" on whatever rules happen to govern our thought (Feser, 2006: 304–305). These rules are not strictly relativistic, because they hinge on evolution, this is an evolution of the CAS that is the mind; but this is, at least in part, a cultural evolution since the mind is a product of social interaction. A cultural evolution that affects the mind and preferences necessarily implies that "human nature" may be influenced by the culture in which it develops.

Feser (2006: 305) explains, "Hayek's view is that those culturally based rules and practices that best enable a group of individuals to adapt to its environment will be those which tend to survive, for the groups that practice them will be the ones which proliferate and the keep the practices alive" (an argument that has led to the view that Hayek favors tradition and even accusations of "social Darwinism," accusations that Hayek refutes in his "Why I Am Not a Conservative," 1960). As Hayek (1988: 21–22) states clearly, "it is less accurate to suppose that man creates and controls his cultural evolution than that it is to say that culture, and evolution, created his reason." If reason is a product of cultural evolution, then human nature is, at least to some extent, a product of culture.

Keeping the Mind Open: Tradition, Markets, and Culture

Although libertarians have claimed Hayek as their own, conservatives argue that his understanding of social evolution and tradition put him squarely in their camp (Scruton, 2006). However, despite Hayek's advocacy for tradition, it would be wrong to conclude that his theoretical work supports traditional religious institutions as necessary, or even appropriate, avenues for spiritual exploration. According to Hayek's spontaneous order theory, the complex system of the mind should not be hampered by the complex system of society, through an imposition of exogenous and imposed rules. Just as the knowledge for the state rests upon a "large sphere independent of majority control in which the opinions of the individuals are formed" (Scruton, 2006: 223), tradition depends upon a large sphere independent of tradition, upon which the experience of the individuals can be formed, and thereby inform the tradition (see Camplin, this volume).

For spontaneous orders of life, mind, and society, we do better not to control the order, but to allow the order to emerge spontaneously. In the case of the mind, this will allow it to expand in ways we cannot predict, but which tighter control would impede, for example, learning. "Thus, by relying on the spontaneous ordering forces, we can extend the scope or range of the order which we may induce to form, precisely because its manifestation will depend on many more circumstances than can be known to us" (Hayek, 1989 [1973]: 41).

Hayek argues that humans convey learning over generations through traditions and customs, as well as through language. "What we call the mind . . . [develops] . . . by absorbing the results of a tradition that is not genetically transmitted" (Hayek, 1988: 22). The system that we call the mind can offer feedback and regulation to the system we call society, and the system of society can act to support and nurture, to "regulate," or to control, the system we call mind. In order for them to remain healthy complex adaptive systems, each system must not be controlled, but can be regulated by feedback from outside of it (Hayek, 1988: 155).[3] This he may have inherited from Ludwig von Mises,

Conservatives argue that Hayek supports tradition, in particular when the tradition goes against rationality, because the tradition carries more information than is available to the individual alone, and even information that the market lacks (Scruton, 2006). This defense of tradition could be used to impose cultural constraints that conflict with an individual's preferences, but Hayek should not be interpreted as arguing that tradition should trump the other systems with which it interacts, including the market, the mind, and common law. Conservatives who interpret Hayek in this way tend to believe more strongly in tradition and custom than in free markets, but this reveal their misunderstanding of Hayek's theory.

For example, Scruton (2006) argues that markets lead to immorality by allowing exchange in areas where he argues that it does not belong; interactions that are moral when there is no exchange of money (e.g., organ donation, sex) are made immoral by its involvement. This, for Scruton, justifies the curbing of markets in these areas. This is related to the Marxian argument that exchange leads to commodification (or, in Marx's terminology, commodity fetishism and alienation). According to Scruton, Hayek's theory supports the case that morality, passed on by tradition, trumps the complex system of the market. Yet, Austrians argue that whether we put a price on something or not, we still aim to reach our ends (Mises, 1949), and money is simply a vehicle for exchange. Money is an emergent property of transactions that we take—it does not direct our actions, but rather acts as an intermediary for exchanges we already were making. Money emerges from our actions, and then acts to regulate the exchanges that follow; however, it does not drive us into moral or immoral actions by its existence[4]. Of course, the earning of money can also incentivize us to do things we might not do for free, but then if the action (providing a kidney, for example) is a moral one, this incentive should be a good thing, according to Austrians, and they have for this reason supported allowing money exchange in these areas.[5]

Hayek argues that markets *are* moral, because they "confer benefits beyond the range of our concrete knowledge" and thus provide "a greater benefit to the community than most direct 'altruistic' action" (Hayek, 1988: 81). Society evolves morality (Hayek, 1960: 35–36). Treating others well, even those with whom we have no face-to-face interactions, helps society evolve in a moral direction. Hayek argues that free interaction in the market allows social evolution and the emergence of new options and freedoms. Money is a vehicle for voluntary transactions, not an evil that promotes commodification of humanity.

Tradition is useful, for Hayek, to convey information helpful for holding society together across generations. Tradition supports common law and the political process, as well as respect for institutions. Tradition can help build trust, which is important for well-functioning markets. Traditions, Hayek argues, "have made constitutions work which did not explicitly state all that they presupposed, or which did not even exist in written form" (1979: 107–108). Tradition aids interactions *between* people, and conveys information *across* generations.

Traditions are only guidelines, and must evolve if they are to be useful. Hence, tradition might, for example, inform us that children are "better raised" when a mother and father commit to each other and marry, but tradition cannot inform us about a *particular situation*. Tradition only provides a guideline, not a uniform law. Just as one should not hear a statistical probability and apply it to any given situation directly, one should not assume that the guideline of tradition directly applies to any given individual. Traditions offer guidance, but should not be taken as rigid rules.

The information that a tradition conveys—that children are "better raised" by married parents—is based upon historical data regarding previous arrangements. Just as prices are historical data, and empirical analysis can only tell us what happened in a particular historical case (Hayek, 1989), tradition conveys information about what worked in the past. Tradition should be no more fixed than prices or common law; as circumstances change, the value of traditions and laws change.

Hence, children may have been raised better by two parents than one in the past, and this may have led to a tradition of marriage between mother and father, but this does not mean that two biological parents today are better equipped to raise a child than a loving same-sex couple, or nonbiological parents who adopt, or a single parent when the other parent is "unfit" or uninterested, for example. Different circumstances in the modern era may produce different selective pressures and outcomes that rightly lead to evolutionary change in flexible institutions. Tradition is limited in what it can convey, and feedback must come from the complex system inside of us, as well as from other free and evolving complex systems, to discern the reliability of the signals coming from inherited tradition. Tradition *passes knowledge* between individuals and across time, but this does not mean that it should *exert limits* upon an individual mind or life.

Hayek did not believe in rational constructivism—imposing a social order upon a society, rather than allowing it to emerge—but he also did not believe in blindly accepting past precedent. Just as common law evolves, tradition evolves, and these evolving institutions must receive interpretation and feedback from the systems around them. The command nature of a hierarchical tradition upon the important choices we make in life today is more similar to civil law instruction than adaptive common law guidelines. The imposition of the rule (marry in order to raise children) upon the internal complex system of the individual (i.e., *be* heterosexual) would be an attempt at exogenously imposed command, or planning, upon a spontaneous order.

Instead, if this complex system (the individual) produces an outcome (e.g., homosexuality) that is inconsistent with tradition, then it should be received as feedback by that order. This is how both the orders (mind and society) evolve and develop. Psychological development of the mind, out of which emerges the individual's preferences and beliefs, comes about as a reflection, in part, of the society in which that mind resides. The CAS of the mind, like the complex system of the market, requires a free area to develop if it is to evolve toward a well-functioning system; and in order to explore the possibility of enlightenment of individual and society, Hayek's theoretical framework should be extended, connecting his cognitive development theories, to his arguments about planned systems.

Free Minds, Free Markets, and the Basic Income Guarantee

Planning of the economy necessitates restrictions on mental freedom. Yet, free markets may also restrict mental freedom. The power to act upon one's free thought will, in a market system, rely upon money: the autonomous power to act. Furthermore, the market system itself may influence an individual's preferences and limit his or her choices in such a way as to reduce his or her psychological freedom and individuality. Individuals are influenced by what those around them purchase, but also the prices and availability of goods are determined by what the most *active* producers and consumers have already purchased (see Nell, 2014a).

The spontaneous order of the system affects the spontaneous order of the mind. Yet if, as David Miller (1989: 129–130) argues, "most of the desires people manifest in market economies are artificially induced," then he is correct that "If markets create the demands that they then proceed to satisfy, the argument [that markets are efficient] becomes damagingly circular." Hayek conceded that culture is an evolutionary process that affects the minds, and by implication the individual preferences, of those within the given evolving system. It would contradict Austrian axioms to postulate that preferences are given outside of societal context. See Nell (this volume) for further discussion of Austrian theory, the individual, and endogenous preferences. Marx (1959 [1844]) believed that human nature would change in his new society; although, just as Austrians predicted, Soviet leaders found that changing the institutions of society by force did not lead to a new development of human nature, we must also recognize the arrogance (or paternalistic attitude), and the ignorance, of assuming that market culture is the only correct one. Also, in a market society, we should recognize the potential for development of the individual's nature toward a monetary distraction and consumerism, and also the development that positive liberty can provide, when it frees the individual to pursue nonmonetary goals.

It is unlikely that individuals will be able to develop themselves if they must spend each day toiling away at a job they do not like, struggling to pay their bills and buy their groceries. Hence, arguably positive liberty is necessary for the all-round development of the individual. Marx and his followers understood this; but libertarians and conservatives who favor free markets frequently argue that the welfare state is detrimental to culture because it removes the incentive to work, and therefore the *drive* to better oneself, and creates instead a "culture of dependency" or "entitlement mentality." The Heritage Foundation has an annually produced Index of Dependence on Government.[6] The libertarian Cato Institute scholar Brink Lindsay recently made the case, in a podcast interview on libertarianism.org, that the generous welfare state in the United Kingdom does this.[7] Does everyone "on the dole" in the United Kingdom, or who is receiving other income support, spend his or her time in unproductive activities? Nell and Richmond (2013) make the case that a basic income, far from leading to laziness and dependency, might be a key part of the transformation of society and development of the individual.

There is no reason to assume that individuals would choose to do nothing useful with their time if they were not forced to work in regular jobs (see Nell and Richmond, 2013).[8] With the cushion a Basic Income Guarantee provides, an individual can retrain, study, start a business, take risks, and try things that he or she would be unable to do without an income to fall back on. In fact, when individuals are made to report to the unemployment office to defend themselves and prove they have been job hunting, taking advantage of the cushion welfare provides is made more difficult, self-esteem is reduced, and so forth. The certainty of a stable Basic Income Guarantee, which would be available whether or not the individual takes on part-time, charitable, or even full-time work, can therefore help unleash entrepreneurial and creative energies.

Finally, what about the psychological desire to have community? Would a free market system, even one supported with a Basic Income Guarantee, still leave something critical out of the picture, leaving the individual psychologically wanting, alone, alienated, and isolated? Marx and his followers have not been alone in their focus upon this component of human nature, and there is a long history of communal activities that have contributed to democracy and a good society (Hirschman, 1996). If we truly desire connection and markets cultivate alienation through their reliance upon individuality, can we build a collective system that could provide the unity that we desire—or would it necessarily become a planned system that reverts to cutting off our spontaneous development and freedom?

The Complexity of Mind and Society

In order to let in the wider mental experience, the complexity of the mind must be respected. Interactions between the various parts of the mind must be allowed, so that new connections and experiences can be formed. Experiences are based on, or at least founded within, the abstractions, and relations between abstractions, of the mind, as networks are formed. Exogenous imposition of ways of thinking will prevent new connections, and hence limit the cognitive flexibility and subjective learning of the individual. This will limit the potential for comprehensive understanding of the social and physical world and for evolution (development) of self and society.

From Hayek's work on spontaneous order, and from complexity theory, or Complex Adaptive Systems (CAS) theory, we know that respecting the complex nature of the mind requires an openness that excludes the imposition of rigid social norms and traditions. For this to be possible, the society—or rather, the state and other powerful groups and institutions, and the people in their capacity to influence culture and opinion—must refrain from planning and enforcing a worldview and preferences on the people for its own purposes, and from imposing rigid and narrow norms for ways of thinking. Instead, an individual should be guided by broad rules, such as moral guidelines, that allow her own understanding of the physical, social, and metaphysical to emerge from within. New ways of thinking, perspectives, and sensory information should be allowed to make contributions to an individual's consciousness. All different parts of the mind should be encouraged to make connections. Rationality and linearity should only be options, rather than rigid limitations upon the mind.

Expectations and traditions meant to frame a "safe" life, as implied by conservatives who have concern for social "maladaptation" if traditions are not closely respected (Scruton, 2006: 219), can go too far not only in social areas such as marriage but also in cognitive areas such as rationality. For example, the importance of art is not merely its entertainment and/or aesthetic value—art can be one way in which connections are made within an open and free mind, allowing the complexity of the mind to produce new emergent thoughts and ideas out of the new connections; education is not merely about learning a trade or advancing science; and intelligence cannot necessarily be quantified with tests and exams. Traditions and boundaries upon the complex system that is consciousness have limited our understanding of our own potential, and economics is among the worst offenders.

Scientists have discovered that new neurons can form (GrandPré, 2007), and new connections are constantly made, over the course of a lifetime. Yet, it is also possible to tread again and again along the same paths, the same narrow range of neural connections made in youth. The ability to learn, and transcend old habits and mistakes, depends upon an openness to new connections and a willingness to forge new neural pathways. New connections are important to new experience and change as a result of life choices and changes, as well as due to changes in perception and consciousness. Consciousness and life are interlinked through perception and experience. An open and evolving consciousness is a precondition of an evolving life: a life capable of betterment.

Perception underlies recognition of opportunity, which can only be subjectively perceived (Hayek, 1945). It is critical to tacit knowledge, innovation, and entrepreneurship, as well as spiritual understanding and wisdom. Perception—for example, for the perceiving of opportunities that Kirzner (2000; 2007 [1963]) discusses—is not objective, definable, and measurable like the five senses, and requires much more than merely use of those senses. Perspective is a result of (1) worldview or ideology, (2) preferences, and (3) framework or set of assumptions and theories used to make sense of new information; and one's perspective defines one's perception. Perception plays an important role in recognizing, seeking out, and accepting changing circumstances so that opportunities can be seen and seized (Kirzner, 2000). A fixed plan, whether of an economy, a community, or an individual life, precludes the seizure of new opportunity; a fixed expectation precludes new awareness. An individual with a set life plan will tend not to perceive other options as they arise, and at the end of the period in question will not even recognize the lost opportunities—the opportunity cost of keeping to this plan. A person must be open to opportunity to recognize it, and for this she must leave her life (somewhat) unplanned over the long term. An open mind allows the individual to perceive and adjust during a period, taking advantage of better options as they arise. Rigid tradition, a conservative outlook, repetition and normality, and "safe" lifelong careers—although seen as a choice, such careers will generally be necessitated by the conditions of the market or made under the duress created by market conditions and the scaffold of tradition that supports it—can prevent the dynamic change necessary for a fulfilling life and an inspiring and entrepreneurial society.

The fear of maladaptation from the social sphere and the consequent (or thereby justified) use of rules of social conduct to impose a certain narrow rationality upon the complex system of mind is an overreach of one system upon another (see Camplin, 2013; and Camplin, this volume). Culture and tradition can be just as coercive as law and legislation. With the punishment of exclusion from society—ostracism—available to them (and Austrians like Leeson, 2009, are well aware of its power), societies can use custom to coerce individuals to, for example, cover themselves from head to toe in black in the desert heat every day for all their lives, keep them locked indoors, and keep them obeying cruel husbands. In fact, having laws to enforce these customs is rarely necessary. Austrians concede the importance of culture, but rarely consider the full implications of this *coercive* power, tending to assume that only the state can coerce the individual.

The individual experience is its own complex system, the rules of which should evolve within the individual, with an evolving sort of "common law of the mind," based on the "trials" of one's life (and the good times), which we learn from and which mold us so that we can survive and thrive. Hayek recognizes that much of the common law of the mind is made up of assumptions and knowledge about the external world, and is tacit and unconscious; Feser (2006) describes Hayek's view, relating it to John Searle, who describes this "background" of consciousness (Feser, 303). [9]. This information must be updated as it changes or as understanding improves; it is a network of hypotheses that are sometimes shown to be wrong, and therefore may change with learning. The background is shaped by social interaction: language frames and experience guides the evolving nature of consciousness.

Subjective knowledge guides consciousness, and the flexibility of the subjective assumptions to new information is critical to attaining the best framework. It is not possible to have objective knowledge of the world (Feser, 2006: 291), to have a perfect framework; hence, the subjective framework that we make do with must be updated as new information becomes available. The complexity of the mind also means that it is difficult to consciously control one's own thoughts: for example, to not think about pink elephants when someone mentions them, to not think depressing or self-conscious thoughts for some, or to forget a painful memory. However, there are still conscious ways to overcome unhealthy perspectives and to transcend the boundaries or constraints that we have on thought. Just as Austrians argue about curing an unhealthy economy, the solution requires not *planning* of the mind, but the *freeing* of it. It does not work to force oneself to think or not think about something, but meditation can help one rise above thoughts and free exploration (e.g., via stream of consciousness or Rorschach tests) can help with discovery, creativity and innovation, and making connections. Planning cannot control the spontaneous order that is the mind, but giving more space to the mind to expand itself can bring about the desired results.

Arguably, the worst consequences of common ownership in the Soviet Union were due to the imposition of the planned order upon a society that had not developed the cultural environment to accept the new order, because the new order had not evolved naturally but had been imposed. Although Lenin expected the people to learn *within* the new institutions (because Marx had argued that economic relations determine human nature), in fact the people needed to be prepared for these new institutions, ready to make democratic use of them, which meant that culture and civil society needed to co-evolve *before* the institutions changed. Absent this, the state had to make the decisions centrally and enforce the laws upon an unwilling public, which led to economic distortions and tyranny (Nell, 2014b).

The spontaneous orders of mind and society have to evolve to the point where the people can accept and work with public property institutions. They need to build new neural pathways a connectionist might suggest, form new habits and norms, based around public property. It is as if they have to be the right "shape" for the new institutions, so that the people and the property laws can fit together like a puzzle, which means they have to be (1) flexible enough first to be able to remold themselves, and then (2) form the right shape. Marxists have continued to criticize capitalism for preventing this flexibility (see, e.g., Adorno and Horkheimer, 1944).

Like Marx's communism, free markets and classical liberalism were intended to allow a flourishing of the individual, but cultural and social freedom have not always come hand in hand with freedom of trade. Religious intolerance, racism, and bigotry of all sorts have often coexisted with an economically free society.[10] Although slavery and legal segregation are gone, American prisons are still disproportionately, even overwhelmingly, filled with minorities (Carson and Golinelli, 2013), who are poorer and far more likely to be stopped by the police ("driving while black," etc.), which is a critical cultural issue whether or not it stems from racism:

> the unequal targeting and treatment of minorities at every stage of the criminal justice process—from arrest to sentencing—reinforces the perception that drives the inequality in the first place, with the unfairness at every successive stage of the process compounding the effects of earlier injustices. The result is a vicious cycle that has evolved into a self-fulfilling prophecy: More minority arrests and convictions perpetuate the belief that minorities commit more crimes, which in turn leads to racial profiling and more minority arrests.[11]

By some measures the American prison system is more expansive than Soviet Gulags (though there are fewer per 100,000 citizens).[12] Although markets can attenuate these social factors, for example, by costing firms profit when they refuse to hire or serve certain people, the market can also offer firms profit to *exclude* a minority if the culture is overwhelmingly racist.

The market is *a*moral: it serves the interests of the culture whether that culture is compassionate and open or violent and racist. And in the United States, in addition to the continuing problem of racism against African Americans, especially in poor areas, there is the relatively new issue of prejudice against Muslim Americans. According to Gallup, "In the U.S., about one-half of nationally representative samples of Mormons,

Protestants, Catholics, Muslims, and Jews agree that in general, most Americans are prejudiced toward Muslim Americans." This is not merely perception: Nearly half of Muslims polled had experienced racial or religious discrimination in the past year.[13]

In the globalized world today, in large developed nations there are many markets serving many subcultures: In some small towns and on some websites, being racist will be profitable, while in others (and on other websites) it will be punished. Racism can also be dissipated through globalization and communication, through getting to know personally those the bias is against. Knowledge of the Islamic religion may or may not reduce discrimination, but getting to know individuals does tend to reduce Islamophobia.[14] This learning through interaction represents a social way for an individual's "background" mental state and preferences to change, and will be reflected in their future interactions. In turn, this can affect the market's reward to firms that discriminate, if those who lose their prejudice use social-turned-economic pressure to help out their new friends.

The market alone cannot be relied upon to encourage moral behavior, and the violent and racist know this, and are well aware of how to coerce businesses. Those who would like to see cultural change in the direction of reduced discrimination and greater compassion and integration should also be aware of how to utilize these social/cultural forces of the market. For change to occur, a cultural movement must *encourage* the private sphere to change; similarly, as Austrians argue, a cultural movement must induce a democratic order to change state law on such matters. The society must change first, and then it can influence the rules in private and public spheres. The libertarian group Students for Liberty recently posted an article encouraging libertarians to prioritize the rights and liberty of lesbian, gay, bisexual, transgendered (LGBT) individuals based on the following argument:

> Libertarianism as a philosophy affirms individual rights and self-ownership. But when discussing self-ownership, the liberty movement far too often only concerns itself with the actual physical body and the fruits of that body's labor. More than tangible objects though, each individual owns his mind, his life, and his happiness. When Bastiat described the essence of man in The Law, he included personality (or in some translations individuality) in addition to liberty and property. While it might seem trite, it is true that each one of us is special and unique, because nobody can ever be you. Self-affirmation and actualization is the prerequisite of a libertarian, free society composed of independent people. In On Liberty, John Stuart Mill wrote that "the free development of individuality is one of the leading essentials of well-being." Far too often, individuals are forced to sacrifice

their essential essence on the altar of conformity in order to get along in society, a situation that should alarm all lovers of liberty.[15]

A market system alone cannot ensure mental and social freedom. There must be a conscious cultural movement toward social libertarianism. Both economic and social systems must provide freedom for the individual mind to develop and express its individuality. So, given that we require social and economic systems that both allow for freedom of their respective CAS, would it be possible to evolve toward a more communal society, or would we necessarily slide back toward authoritarianism? What if, as a society, we advance our understanding of social systems and of our own minds, through exploration of theories of the mind as a CAS, is it possible that the evolution of our own enlightenment might make this cultural-social evolution more possible?

COMPLEXITY, RELIGION, AND TRANSCENDING THE SELF

Hayek was agnostic, but his neural network approach to understanding human consciousness (Gauss, 2006) and his understanding of the mind as a spontaneous order (Hayek, 1952; Gauss, 2006: 250), intimately connected to culture and "feeding back" into culture (Gauss, 2006: 251), reveal his approach to consciousness and society and also provide a basic structure upon which to analyze the mind-body problem and perhaps even metaphysical or spiritual questions.[16]

As Gerald Gauss (2006) explains in the *Cambridge Companion to Hayek*, Hayek argues that the mind emerges from the complex system of neurons, and their vast numbers and types of interactions. The connections between neural clusterings that compose the complex system of the mind, and its representation of the self to the conscious mind, are made by connecting symbolic interpretations of experiences, none of which are actual experiences of the external world. Hayek argues that, therefore, there is no basis to believe that the representation of physical reality that the mind makes possible is a complete representation of the world. There is an opening within this framework for an understanding of the world that could be described as religious or spiritual.

This understanding of the mind, neural networks, and connectionism, and its implications for the self, and for metaphysical questions, is profound and important. Unfortunately, Hayek's application of these insights focuses mainly on the role of the mind, rationality, and rules for forming social behavior, not upon the complexity of mind and experience for its *own* purposes: spiritual or individual enlightenment, which in turn might "feed back," allowing for social enlightenment, as Marx and his followers believed possible. However, looking closely at his theories, we can infer metaphysical implications.

The mind, according to Hayek, "does not so much make rules as *consist* of rules" (1973: 18). The conscious mind must be guided by a set of unconscious rules. The nonconscious parts of the mind are not necessarily subconscious (1978c: 45), but may be superconscious. Rules govern the conscious process, but we cannot be aware of these rules consciously: to consciously know these rules, this conscious awareness would have to be governed by a higher set of rules. To know those rules, this higher mental consciousness must be ruled by yet a higher set. Hence, the mind cannot consciously know itself completely. "The whole idea of the mind explaining itself is [thus] a logical contradiction" (1952: 192).

However, although we cannot be rationally aware of the infinite, we may be able to become one with it, and experience it unconsciously. God is said to be greater than that which can be conceived intellectually or consciously (see also Johnson, 1965). This is the same thing that Hayek said of the mind: it cannot know itself because it is greater than that which can be consciously perceived. Our inability to know our own mind may appear to us religiously as God.[17] This would underlie our continued, ongoing frustration about the divide between self and other, finite and infinite, individual and universal consciousness, mind and body. This is the same divide that Marx so adamantly believed that his communist system would help society to overcome. Today, researchers are using cutting-edge techniques in cognitive neuroscience to study philosophy of mind and metaphysics (Sprevak and Kallestrup, 2014).

Marx (1959 [1844]) also described a sort of universal consciousness and transcendence of self, yet he described it as something that could and must be accomplished outside of the self, in the social sphere. The transcendence of private property and individualism would offer new freedom and a new human nature.[18] When society reached the "end of history" and transcended capitalism to take on collective ownership of property and rationally and consciously direct production as a society, the division between self and other would also be overcome. Because this "return of man to himself" is "accomplished consciously and embracing the entire wealth of previous development," it would lead to that great prosperity Marx spoke of, in which "all the springs of co-operative wealth flow more abundantly." Therefore, Marx predicted "the genuine resolution of the conflict between man and nature and between man and man" (Marx, 1959).

Metaphysically and physically, Marx saw the new society as a great transcendence of the challenges of history. It was man consciously transcending a system that had incredible wealth but also incredible divisions, in which some had exploited others in order to produce that wealth. Hence, the new system would be "the true resolution of the strife between existence and essence, between objectification and self-confirmation, between freedom and necessity, between the individual and the species." Marx (1959 [1844]) sums this up, saying: "Communism is the riddle of history solved, and it knows itself to be this solution."[19]

Marx's morality has distinct spiritual, or metaphysical, elements. Although Marxists often decried religion and metaphysics, their own theory was highly metaphysical, predicting the transcendence of self and other, and the resolution of existence and essence, and it outlined an ethics that is not dissimilar to religious moral law (Bax, 1893; Nell, 2014a), and that has been characterized as a "secular" religion (e.g., Boyan, 1968; Rothbard, 1990). Marx argues that this transcendence can be reached through the enlightenment of the society, or the species. Hayek (1974) argues that because social scientists are trying to understand processes more complex than themselves, than their own minds are able to comprehend, they cannot ever produce the kind of knowledge a natural scientist can produce. An enlightened society would understand this issue, and come to a solution that works *with* the spontaneous orders of democracy (governance), market (exchange), culture (tradition), mind (consciousness), and technology (advance of abundance), just as Nell (2014b) argues that the Soviet leadership needed to do.

With this enlightenment, perhaps the people could come together to stand up for what they believe in, together, without being an angry crowd (see Camplin, 2013: 101 and Camplin, this volume, for an Austrian view of mob behavior), but instead through enlightened, transparent, open and nonhierarchical discussion and agreement (see also Nell, this volume; Nell, 2014a). Neither hierarchical command decisions nor self-interested individualistic decisions would rule, but instead a public conversation could lead to outcomes that serve a community holistically.

It we truly desire connection and collective living and unity, can the void unfilled by markets, which cultivates alienation through individuality, instead be filled by a collective system that allows the unity that we desire? Or does it require a unity that is beyond our nature? If the culture and society evolve before or concurrently with institutional change, it may be possible. If the individual has a greater area of internal freedom, so that he or she is able to express individualism and "natural" preferences that develop in a cultural evolution driven by an enhancing freedom of expression and societal response (democratic and market based) to this self-expression, then a more "natural" interaction between society and the individual mind might drive the evolutionary change and allow for the emergence of a collective society that does not require planning or limitations upon psychological freedom.

The physical world, Hayek argues, is unknowable by the mind directly, but can only be known through abstracted symbolic connections, and the mind cannot know itself completely due to the problem of infinite regress (to know each level of consciousness requires a higher one). Yet, the mind is a network of neural connections—physical wiring of the brain. Hayek argues that "in some ultimate sense mental phenomena are 'nothing but' physical processes," but "we will never be able to dispense with the use of mental terms [for] we shall never be able to explain [them] in terms of physical laws" (1952: 191). Our minds, "must remain irreducible entities" or systems. (1989: 86–87). The mind that we "cannot know" has emerged from the physical. The fact that we cannot know it may explain why it is irreducible to a physical explanation.

Many metaphysical and scientific descriptions of levels of consciousness exist. One way in which one can reach a higher level, it is argued, is by transcending the ego or self. Hayek argues that the self is constituted in social experience, through neural connections—whether we plod along the same old pathways of our youth or whether we break free from them to forge new kinds of experience and learning. If the self is so constituted, then it should be possible to transcend, as Eastern philosophy argues, by overcoming the limitations of these social relations, and reforging the neural pathways outside of these well-trodden paths and networks. This also forms the basis of the "liberative model" of (psychological) development, which is founded upon these Eastern philosophical traditions because of their direct focus on transcending the self (Levenson, Aldwin, and Cupertino, 2001).

The mind we cannot know is an emergent system, and it sets the context for later connections. The mind is produced by the micro-level activity and connections, and the micro-level activity is in turn constrained by the dynamic system. Local interactions of the parts, just as in the market, give rise to a global dynamic pattern and, in turn, this global dynamic sets the context in which future local connections occur (Hayek, 1989: 93). It is cyclical, ongoing, evolutionary development, as any complex adaptive system (CAS) or spontaneous order must be. Neither comes first—the micro or the macro—they are integrated and interdependent.

There are two things to consider in Hayek's arguments with regard to whether transcendence is possible, and what it may constitute metaphysically. First, Hayek makes the case that the mind cannot consciously know itself (1952: 167); however, the spiritual experience of transcending the self and reaching enlightenment may not be "conscious" in the usual sense. Second, Hayek's argument is that consciously knowing the rules that govern the mind requires the operation of a higher order consciousness with a new set of rules that guide it. At each level, the understanding of a given order's rules presupposes a higher order consciousness with its own set of rules: These may be what are known as levels of spiritual consciousness or awareness (Hayek recognized the distinction between consciousness and the mind, with a theory of the subconscious; Hayek, 1952: 132).

Some philosophers of spirituality and "Vedic psychology" base their theories upon a similar connectionist understanding of the mind, and include a "transcendental Self" as one higher level of consciousness and "Progressively more abstract and subtle levels of mind display greater capacity to order and integrate experience" (Nidich, Nidich, and Alexander, 2000). Some levels of the mind may lie outside of conscious awareness. However, they can be reached, and one's ultimate transcendence of the self entirely allows one to reach spiritual enlightenment and unity with the universe (Cook-Greuter, 2000).

The finite mind cannot know itself perhaps because its whole self is the universal consciousness or part of the fabric of an infinite universe, and the finite cannot know the infinite; however, perhaps the infinite can be experienced through the finite, with metaphysical transcendence (van Riessen, 2007). This unity with the universe, or Other or God or infinity, (Proudfoot, 1975; Long, 2006; van Riessen, 2007), or the "underlying seamless Reality," as Cook-Greuter calls it, is not experienced consciously, because it cannot be put into language. "Hence we face the inevitable paradox of trying to express with words that which is ineffable and beyond any conjecture we can make about it from our limited perspective" (Cook-Greuter, 2000: 232). Although this process of individual enlightenment involves transcending the self (see the levels of ego-development outlined in Cook-Greuter, 2000: 230) and might sound like a personal spiritual experience, it is not actually an individual or personal experience separate from culture and society. The self is a social construct, but more than this, to transcend the self means to overcome (or transcend) the *limitations imposed by culture,* which make up the ego of the "lower levels" of ego-development as Cook-Greuter defines it.

The "construct-aware" ego stage of the Cook-Greuter system is a level quite near to the fully transcendent self, and "it is at this juncture that people first become aware of how reality is both perceived and constructed through the filter of patterned thought and language" (2000: 232–233)[20]. This realization—something with which of course Austrians would agree—is part of Cook-Greuter's stages of ego-development, or as Marxists and post-Austrian market socialists call it, "enlightenment" (see Nell, 2014b). Cook-Greuter's criteria for transcendence levels for ego-development read like a description of Austrian methodology. Before reaching transcendence (enlightenment), one must learn to see the world more holistically, to transcend the culture's fixed and imposed consciousness, and must recognize the flexibility of the complex system that is consciousness and perception—the complex system of the mind must attempt to know itself:

> To see reality as well as the self as an interconnected whole or system rather than an aggregate of separate, well-defined elements is the first step towards a more holistic view of reality.
>
> The main advantage of the system over the conventional, linear view is that people now realize that their perspectives are *local, partial, context-dependent and culturally conditioned.* (Cook-Greuter, 2000: 234, my emphasis)

These—local, partial, context-dependent and culturally conditioned—sound, in other words, like subjectivity with local-tacit knowledge, constrained knowledge or incomplete information, in a path-dependent cyclical system with endogenous elements. So, Cook-Greuter is essentially saying that we all must come to recognize that we are as (post) Austrian economists describe us, but that, through recognition of this, we can become as Marxists would like us to be. If we as a society can become enlightened, can come to know ourselves, perhaps we can develop our nature and our culture, and (as discussed in Nell, this volume) build a better democracy and society, with less bureaucracy and rent-seeking and more civil service, community, public conversation, and creative collaboration.

Conclusion

Psychological development of the mind and individual preferences and beliefs develop as a reflection of the society in which that mind resides. The isolated individualism of a market economy is damaging and distorts the CAS of the mind in a different way than the more united but also more hierarchical planned economy. Is there a way to allow the free development of mind and society that is not alienating and isolating for the individual, that allows individuals to form social bonds as well as transcend their socially constructed selves? Is it possible for individuals and society to reach enlightenment, and what would this mean for our global future?

The natural extension of Hayek's arguments on complexity and planning extend to his cognitive development theories. Although this area needs much more development, there are very interesting overlaps between Hayek's work on spontaneous orders and the field of connectionist philosophy and developmental psychology, and these even help bridge Hayek and Marx. Hayek's work on the internal (psychological) and external (social) systems should be joined and explored for their insights on individual and social enlightenment, which was a goal set by Marx but which should be desirable to all.

NOTES

1. Although some have criticized the extension of economics to analyze all kinds of social interaction, arguably if it is the tools but not the content of the economic science that is extended, in order to analyze morality, psychology, and other areas of social study, it can expand our understanding of social science rather than reducing it all to economic consideration. This will be explored more below.
2. Bolshevik leader and Marxist theoretician Nikolai Bukharin (1921) described the difference between the way in which the market fulfilled the desires of individuals and the way in which the planned society would. He asks: what is the relation between the price and the price that each individual in the society would wish for? In the market, Bukharin argues, "It is obvious that the price will not coincide with these wishes. For many persons this price will be outright ruinous; namely, for those who simply cannot buy anything 'at such prices.'" In the "organized society," however, there are no "contradictions between personal and social interests" because "We are now dealing with a friendly brotherhood of workers with a common plan for production." http://www.marxists.org/archive/bukharin/works/1921/histmat/2.htm.
3. After quoting the above section from Hayek, regarding what is not genetically transmitted, Gary Dempsey of the Cato Institute writes: "This 'memetic' view not only provides a mechanism for minds to limit/correct catastrophic errors in society, but for society to limit/correct catastrophic errors in the mind. In other words, the system that we call the mind can act to 'regulate' the system of society and the system of society can act to 'regulate' the system that we call the mind. Moreover, when these systems are taken as one, this larger system can act in 'self-regulating' ways." Cato White Papers and Miscellaneous Reports: "Hayek's Evolutionary Epistemology, Artificial Intelligence, and the Question of Free Will," by Gary T. Dempsey, http://www.cato.org/pubs/wtpapers/hayekee.html
4. The ability to purchase on the market something previously reserved to a nonmarket realm is simply a new freedom: it represents a choice, to

purchase the product or service or to refrain from doing so. If the product or service should be seen as immoral, its availability lends one's morality a deeper value. The active choice to be moral is more meaningful than morality due to coercion or necessity (e.g., Kant's *Metaphysics of Morals*). Hence, even the availability of "immoral" substances need not itself be seen as immoral, just the use of them.

5. These Austrians have not convincingly addressed the concern that the extreme poor may be driven to sell their organs out of desperation, leaving them worse off, but have responded by arguing that their actions are voluntarily and that they are better off choosing to take such actions if it keeps them from starving, which presumably is what drove them to such extreme measures in the first place.
6. Produced in November 2013, the most recent one is here: http://www.heritage.org/research/reports/2013/11/the-2013-index-of-dependence-on-government.
7. "Is Inequality a Problem?" featuring Brink Lindsey, Aaron Ross Powell, and Trevor Burrus: http://www.libertarianism.org/media/free-thoughts-podcast/is-income-inequality-problem.
8. J. K. Rowling famously wrote her Harry Potter book series while "on the dole," and many musicians and artists in the United States and United Kingdom have produced their early work while receiving income assistance. After all, not everyone can produce great works with only evening and weekends to work on them, especially if the only paid work they can find is exhausting or they have a family or other things in their life that also require their time. Relieving money stresses can unleash artistic creativity, and most people get bored with being unproductive after a little while. With a Basic Income Guarantee, they could then either voluntarily return to work, engage in creative pursuits, or volunteer in charitable activities.
9. "All intentional mental states, [Searle says], have the content they do only by virtue of their place in a vast "Network" (Searle intends this as a technical term) of intentional states. The desire to run for the presidency of the United States, for example, has the intentional content it has only in the context of such other intentional states as the belief that the United States has presidential elections, the desire that people cast votes for you, and so on. But this Network of intentional states functions against a "Background" (another technical term) of capacities which are themselves non-intentional. Such capacities will for most people include, for example, the presupposition that there is an external physical world" (Feser, 2006: 303).
10. The First Amendment in the United States did not prevent the censoring and imprisonment of anyone distributing information about birth control, and textbooks mentioning the subject were burned explicitly for religious-cultural reasons, during the heyday of the Comstock Laws. Many of these laws stayed in force through until the 1960s. One report from Anthony Comstock lists the items seized under this law: "Book and sheet stock seized and destroyed: 52 pounds. Obscene pictures and photos: 19,260. Negative plates for making obscene photos: 842. Articles for immoral use

of rubber, etc.: 1,000. Boxes of pills and powders used by abortionists: 66. Circulars, catalogs, songs, poems, etc.: 7,891. Newspapers containing unlawful advertisements or obscene matter: 22. Obscene pictures framed on walls of saloons: 7. Obscene plays stopped or places of amusement closed: 1." https://www.nytimes.com/books/first/p/petersen-sex.html

11. "Racial Disparities in the American Criminal Justice System" by Ronald Weich and Carlos Angulo. http://urbanpoverty.qwriting.qc.cuny.edu/files/2011/01/Ronald-Weich-and-Carlos-Angulo-Racial-Disparities-in-the-American-Criminal-Justice-System.pdf.
12. The article famously making this case, and offering disturbing counts regardless of this comparison, is "The Caging of America: Why Do We Lock Up So Many People?" Adam Gopnik, *The New Yorker*, January 30, 2012, http://www.newyorker.com/magazine/2012/01/30/the-caging-of-america

    See further discussion and comparisons here: Sean's Russia Blog, "US Prison Industrial Complex versus the Stalinist State". http://seansrussiablog.org/2013/05/11/us-prison-industrial-complex-versus-the-stalinist-gulag/.
13. "Specifically, 66% of Jewish Americans and 60% of Muslim Americans say that Americans in general are prejudiced toward Muslim Americans." Also: "Muslims (48%) are more likely than Americans of other major religious groups to say they, personally, have experienced racial or religious discrimination in the past year. Muslim Americans are more than twice as likely as U.S. Jews, Catholics, and Protestants to say they experienced such discrimination in the past year." See http://www.gallup.com/poll/157082/islamophobia-understanding-anti-muslim-sentiment-west.aspx?version=print.
14. According to Gallup, Americans with some (self-reported) knowledge of Islam are more likely to say they are prejudiced against it than those with just a little or no knowledge; however, in a section "Addressing Islamophobia by Bringing People Closer Together," Gallup reports that people who live in "isolated" communities, with no contact with Muslims, are more likely to have negative views about Islam and to say that Muslims are sympathetic to al Qaeda. See http://www.gallup.com/poll/157082/islamophobia-understanding-anti-muslim-sentiment-west.aspx?version=print.
15. The original posting on Students for Liberty is no longer available, but a reprint can be found here: http://www.txwclp.org/2012/05/shackles-of-conformity/.
16. Although this section may seem to reach beyond social and economic questions, this book is primarily about, and even seem to speculate wildly about, spiritual matters, the flexibility of consciousness discussed here is founded in Hayek's work and has importance for questions of individuality, self and society, and culture. If Hayek's work can show the way to spiritual enlightenment, it may also help us reach social enlightenment, which may pave the way for a new society that can overcome the issues (from bureaucracy and rent-seeking to shirking and moral hazard to the corruption of power-seeking and control) created by "human nature," which thus far have prevented common ownership societies from prospering. Perhaps this is unrealistic and utopian, but this should not prevent the scholar from investigating the issues and exploring the theories that have any, however

remote, chance of finding answers, and a pathway to success. If we can imagine—in popular culture—a future society that has defeated the worst problems of greed and violence—which emerged amid scarcity but continued to thrive amid much more plenty—why not explore whether this utopian future could one day actually be realized?

17. Connecting this to the mind-body problem, we know that the physical world of the brain is the same physical world as that of the universe. Hence, knowing this unknowable mind could be to transcend the physical world of the brain and join the greater physical world of the universe outside ourselves, or to reach enlightenment. In other words, to fully know the system that has emerged from the physically delineated object we call the brain, would be to reach the boundary of this physical separation and come to know the nature of the physical universe. This would be the "universal consciousness," the unity of the self and other, the one mind reaching unity with the God-self.
18. Just as Marx argued that the "estrangement" produced by private property corroded society in the capitalist system, the theory of "making socialists" argued that human nature would be transformed by living in the socialist society. This theory of cultural evolution provided an answer to the argument made by critics of socialism that the natural selfishness of man would destroy the socialist society. Bolshevik leaders explicitly relied upon this transformation within their theory.
19. Full text can be found here: www.marxists.org/archive/marx/works/1844/manuscripts/comm.htm.
20. Cook-Greuter points out that Zen Buddhism "has developed a methodology, the so-called "koan," by which students are confronted with their attachment to discursive reasoning. Essentially the koan is a paradox, i.e., that which is "beyond" (Gk. *para*) "thinking" (Gk., *dokein*), and transcends the logical or conceptual. Since the koan eludes solution by means of reasoning, it requires a quantum leap to another level of comprehension beyond the logical contradictions and the dualistic splits inherent in language" (238).

References

Adorno, Theodor and Max Horkheimer. 1944. "The Culture Industry: Enlightenment as Mass Deception." In Adorno and Horkheimer's *The Dialectic of Enlightenment*, at http://www.marxists.org/reference/archive/adorno/1944/culture-industry.htm.

Bax, E. Belfort. 1893. *The Ethics of Socialism.* London & New York: Swan Sonnenschein.

Boyan, Stephen A. Jr. 1968. "Defining Religion in Operational and Institutional Terms." *University of Pennsylvania Law Review*, 116(3): 479–498.

Bukharin, Nikolai. 1925 [1921]. *Historical Materialism: A System of Sociology.* New York: International Publishers.

Camplin, Troy. 2013. "BIG and the Negative Income Tax: A Comparative Spontaneous Orders Approach." In Guinevere L. Nell (ed.), *Basic Income and the Free Market: Austrian Economics and the Potential for Efficient Redistribution*, 97–122. New York: Palgrave Macmillan.

Carson, E. Ann, and Daniela Golinelli. 2013. *Sentenced State and Federal Prisoners, by Sex, Race, Hispanic Origin, and Age*. Washington, DC: US Dept. of Justice Bureau of Justice Statistics.

Cook-Greuter, Susanne R. 2000. "Mature Ego Development: A Gateway to Ego Transcendence?" *Journal of Adult Development*, 7(4): 227–240 .

Dempsey, Gary T. 1996. "Hayek's Evolutionary Epistemology, Artificial Intelligence, and the Question of Free Will." *Evolution and Cognition*, 2(2): 139–150.

Feser, Edward. 2006. "Hayek the Cognitive Scientist and Philosopher of Mind." In Edward Feser (ed.), *The Cambridge Companion to Hayek*. Cambridge: Cambridge University Press.

Gauss, Gerald F. 2006. "Hayek on the Evolution of Society and Mind." In Edward Feser (ed.), *The Cambridge Companion to Hayek*. Cambridge: Cambridge University Press.

GrandPré, T. 2007. "Adult Neurogenesis: Do New Neurons Develop in the Brain?" *BioEd Online*, March 21, http://www.bioedonline.org/hot-topics/adult-neurogenesis.cfm.

Hayek, F. A. 1945. "The Use of Knowledge in Society." *The American Economic Review*, 35(4): pp. 519–530.

———. 1952. *The Sensory Order*. Chicago: The University of Chicago Press.

———. 1960. *The Constitution of Liberty*. Chicago: University of Chicago Press.

———. 1973. *Rules and Order, Vol I: Law, Legislation, and Liberty*. London: Routledge and Kegan Paul.

———. 1974. "The Pretence of Knowledge." Prize Lecture: Lecture to the memory of Alfred Nobel, December 11, 1974, http://www.nobelprize.org/nobel_prizes/economic-sciences/laureates/1974/hayek-lecture.html.

———. 1978a. *New Studies in Philosophy, Politics, Economics, and the History of Ideas*. London: Routledge.

———. 1978b. *The Errors of Constructivism. New Studies in Philosophy, Politics, Economics and the History of Ideas*. Chicago: University of Chicago Press.

———. 1978c. *The Primacy of the Abstract. New Studies in Philosophy, Politics, Economics and the History of Ideas*. Chicago: University of Chicago Press.

———. 1988. *The Fatal Conceit: The Errors of Socialism*, Chicago: University of Chicago Press.

———. 1989 [1973]. *Law, Legislation, and Liberty*, Vol. I. New York and London: Routledge & Kegan Paul.

———. 1989 [1974]. "The Pretence of Knowledge." *The American Economic Review*, 79(6): 3–7.

Huxley, Aldous. 1969. *Brave New World*. New York: Harper Perennial.

Hirschman, Albert. 1996. "Melding the Public and the Private Spheres: Taking Commensality Seriously." *Critical Review*, 10(4): 533–550 .

Johnson, Oliver A. 1965. "God and St. Anselm." *The Journal of Religion*, 45(4): 326–334.

Kirzner, Israel. 2007 [1963]. *Market Theory and the Price System*. Auburn, AL: The Mises Institute.

———. 2000. *The Driving Force of the Market: Essays in Austrian Economics*, London: Routledge.

Leeson, Peter. 2009. "The Laws of Lawlessness." *The Journal of Legal Studies* 38(2): 471–503.

Levenson, M. R., Aldwin, C. M., and Cupertino, A. P. 2001. "Transcending the Self: Toward a Liberative Model of Adult Development." In A. L. Neri (ed.), *Maturidade & velhice: Um enfoque multidisclinar*, 99–116. Sao Paulo, BR: Papirus.

Long, Eugene Thomas. 2006. "Self and Other: An Introduction." *International Journal for Philosophy of Religion*, 60: 1–7.

Marx, Karl. 1959 [1844]. *The Economic and Philosophic Manuscripts*. Moscow: Progress Publishers.

McCann, C. R. 2002. "F. A. Hayek: The Liberal as Communitarian." *The Review of Austrian Economics*, 15(1): 5–34.

Miller, David. 1989a. *Market, State, and Community*. Oxford: Oxford University Press.

Mises, Ludwig von. 1966 [1949]. *Human Action: A Treatise on Economics*. San Francisco: Fox and Wilkes. http://mises.org/Books/humanaction.pdf.

Nell, Guinevere Liberty. 2014a. "The Post-Austrian School and the New Market Socialism." In *Austrian Theory and Economic Organization: Reaching Beyond Free Market Boundaries*. New York: Palgrave.

———. 2014b. *Spontaneous Order and the Utopian Collective*. New York: Palgrave.

———. 2013. "Welfare in the Austrian Marketplace: Bridging Austrian and Market Socialist Economics." In Guinevere Liberty Nell (ed.), *Basic Income and the Free Market: Austrian Economics and the Potential for Efficient Redistribution*, pp. 7–48. New York: Palgrave Macmillan.

———. 2010. Rediscovering Fire: Basic Economic Lessons from the Soviet Experiment. New York: Algora.

Nell, Guinevere Liberty and Daniel Richmond. 2013. "A BIG Paradigm Shift for Society: A Speculative Look at Some of the Implications of introducing a BIG." In Guinevere Liberty Nell (ed.), *Basic Income and the Free Market: Austrian Economics and the Potential for Efficient Redistribution*, pp. 7–48. New York: Palgrave Macmillan.

Nidich, Sanford I., Randi J. Nidich, and Charles N. Alexander. 2000. "Moral Development and Higher States of Consciousness." *Journal of Adult Development* 7(4): 217–225.

Pols, Edward. 1999. "Knowing God Directly." *International Journal for Philosophy of Religion* 45: 31–49.

Proudfoot, Wayne, 1975. "Conceptions of God and the Self," *The Journal of Religion*, 55(1): 57–75.

Rothbard, Murray N. 1990. "Karl Marx: Communist as Religious Eschatologist." *The Review of Austrian Economics* 4(1): 123–179.
Scruton, Roger. 2006. "Hayek and Conservatism." In Edward Feser (ed.), *The Cambridge Companion to Hayek*, pp. 208–231. Cambridge, United Kingdom: Cambridge University Press.
Sprevak, Mark, and Jesper Kallestrup (eds.). 2014. *New Waves in Philosophy of Mind*. New York: Palgrave Macmillan.
van Riessen, Renée D. N. 2007. *Man as a Place of God: Levinas' Hermeneutics of Kenosis*. Dordrecht, Netherlands: Springer.

List of Contributors

Corey Abel is a writer and editor living in Denver, Colorado. He has taught political theory and humanities at Colorado College, the University of Colorado, and elsewhere. He is the author of articles on Michael Oakeshott's relationship to Aristotle, and his ideas on religion and art, and has edited two collections of essays on Oakeshott.

Troy Camplin is a consultant at Camplin Creative Consulting and an independent scholar.

Andy Denis is Senior Lecturer in Political Economy in the Department of Economics, City University London. He teaches financial economics, fiscal strategy, money and banking, and history of economic thought. His research area is the history and philosophy of economics. He received his PhD in 2002 with a thesis on collective and individual rationality, and has published on Adam Smith, Keynes, Malthus, Hayek, epistemology and policy prescription, the methodology of the Austrian school, and the neoclassical concept of equilibrium. He is currently working on methodological individualism, the microfoundations debate, and the socialist calculation debate.

Gus diZerega holds a PhD in Political Theory, with international teaching and publishing experience in academia focusing on political and environmental theory and policy. His most recent book *Faultlines: The Sixties, Culture War and the Return of the Divine Feminine* was published in 2013.

Leslie Marsh is Senior Researcher in the Faculty of Medicine, The University of British Columbia.

Guinevere Liberty Nell studied and published in the areas of Austrian economics, economic policy, and Soviet economic history, and worked as tax policy analyst for five years at the Heritage Foundation in Washington DC, before earning a master's degree in Soviet economic history from the

University of Warwick, UK. She is the author of *Rediscovering Fire: Basic Economic Lessons from the Soviet Experiment* and *Spontaneous Order and The Utopian Collective*, and editor of *Basic Income and the Free Market: Austrian Economics and the Potential for Efficient Redistribution* and *Austrian Theory and Economic Organization.*

Index

GPSR Compliance
The European Union's (EU) General Product Safety Regulation (GPSR) is a set of rules that requires consumer products to be safe and our obligations to ensure this.

If you have any concerns about our products, you can contact us on

ProductSafety@springernature.com

In case Publisher is established outside the EU, the EU authorized representative is:

Springer Nature Customer Service Center GmbH
Europaplatz 3
69115 Heidelberg, Germany

www.ingramcontent.com/pod-product-compliance
Lightning Source LLC
Chambersburg PA
CBHW072302280926
52266CB00004B/75
* 9 7 8 1 1 3 7 3 7 1 4 0 9 *